ORDINARY GOODNESS

ORDINARY GOODNESS

The Surprisingly Effortless Path to Creating a Life of Meaning and Beauty

Edward Viljoen

A TarcherPerigee Book

tarcherperigee
An imprint of Penguin Random House LLC
375 Hudson Street
New York, New York 10014

Library of Congress Cataloging-in-Publication Data

Names: Viljoen, Edward, author.
Title: Ordinary goodness : the surprisingly effortless path to creating a life of meaning and beauty / Edward Viljoen.
Description: New York : TarcherPerigee, [2017]
Identifiers: LCCN 2016029449 | ISBN 9780399183911 (pbk.)
Subjects: LCSH: Conduct of life. | Good and evil. | Spiritual life.
Classification: LCC BJ1589 .V55 2017 | DDC 170/.44—dc23

Printed in the United States of America
1 3 5 7 9 10 8 6 4 2

Book design by Katy Riegel

Contents

Part Three: Ordinary Compassion

Part Four: Ordinary Faith

Part Five: Finding Faith

Introduction

There is a light in the soul, Meister Eckhart wrote—a light that is uncreated and that cannot be created.* I call that light "ordinary goodness," and I believe that the ultimate goal of life, if there is such a thing, is to express that goodness by letting it come alive in us. However, goodness, like love, makes us exposed and vulnerable. Yet we can no more withdraw from our natural-born goodness than we can withdraw from our inclination to love—not if we expect to live a life of meaning and worth.

C. S. Lewis, in *The Four Loves*, warns that

> *To love at all is to be vulnerable. Love anything and your heart will be wrung and possibly broken. If you want to make sure of keeping it intact, you must give it to no one, not even an animal. Wrap it carefully round with hobbies and little luxuries; avoid all entanglements. Lock it up safe in the casket or coffin of your selfishness. But in that casket, safe, dark, motionless,*

---

* Meister Eckhart, *Selected Writings* (New York: Penguin Books, 1994), 133.

*airless, it will change. It will not be broken; it will become unbreakable, impenetrable, and irredeemable. To love is to be vulnerable.**

Goodness is everything from love, gentle kindness, compassion, and generosity to moral distinction or virtue. It is strength and excellence and sometimes, as we will see later, a synonym for the Divine. Most importantly, I believe, goodness is already present in us, like a dormant seed waiting for the right circumstances to germinate and then take root. Moreover, when it does, it has immense power to inspire and instill hope, to help and nurture. When we do not allow it to spring forth, the consequences are worrisome—for a life not fueled by ordinary goodness must draw its strength from somewhere else. And the options are grim.

I use the word "ordinary" to describe goodness, both in the sense of something unexceptional—of no particular interest—as well as in the sense of something so normal that it goes easily unnoticed. Mainstream news services report on life's spectacular and alarming events, the horrific and the surprising, while all the time regular people everywhere continue to give expression to enormous amounts of ordinary goodness when they awkwardly love their child, quietly recover from a setback, take out the trash for a neighbor even though they are pressed for time, show up uncomfortably at an acquaintance's mother's memorial, or donate to a cause when personal resources are low—all without fanfare or special announcement. Goodness is so ordinary that it is not newsworthy, as some news services that cover good news have discovered. Their focus on goodness falls into the background, drowned out by sensational stories of danger and wrongdoing—the type of stories that attract readers and, therefore, advertisers.†

* C. S. Lewis, *The Four Loves* (New York: Harvest Books, 1971).

† See the appendix for news services that focus on reporting good news.

Viktoria Nekrasova, of the Russian-language online news service The City Reporter, tells on her Facebook page what happened when her agency's site attempted to feature positive angles on the stories in the daily stream for one day. "It turned out that virtually nobody wants it," she wrote, noting that the site drew significantly fewer readers that day.

Why, then, the fascination in social media with puppies and cats, babies, selfies, random acts of kindness, and stories about love overcoming just about everything? Because ordinary goodness is not dead. It is just ordinary. For goodness to become fascinating, the habit of *not* noticing it must be interrupted. Goodness must be cherished and enjoyed, resolutely and mindfully. When we do that, we may begin an extraordinary journey of discovery on which attention to goodness inevitably leads to the expression of everyday kindness. And kindness, when nurtured, develops compassion. And compassion will bring us face-to-face with life's paradoxes and contradictions, and that, in turn, will bring us back to the starting point of our journey: goodness, with a new question. Is goodness worth it? That is where faith comes in. Not faith of a religious kind, although that will work too, but faith in the sense of trusting what cannot be logically explained: our inclination to goodness, even though it gives very few guarantees and seems riddled with inconsistencies.

The Benefits of This Book

Ordinary Goodness consists of five parts. The first four are Ordinary Goodness, Ordinary Kindness, Ordinary Compassion, and Ordinary Faith. It offers stories and practices to illustrate how to explore and express these qualities more powerfully in life. The fifth part of this book shifts focus to finding your own faith by examining what you believe. In this last part, I share what I have come to believe, not as a way of explaining the meaning of life, but as an illustration of what I think all people ought to find for themselves. Throughout this book, you will find suggestions for your application, titled "practice."

Meister Eckhart wrote that there is something in the soul so akin to the Divine that it is one with the Divine, and this "something" has nothing in common with anything created. Your goodness may be ordinary, yet it exists in you in a unique and unrepeatable way. It is to that ordinary state of goodness in all people that I dedicate this book. That "something" nudges and prods us to live in sync with it, and it will not let us rest when we ignore it.

A Role Model for Ordinary Goodness

For Goodness' Sake

I think of my grandmother when people tell me I am a good listener. I think of her when people say any good thing about me. When I act courageously or comfort someone in distress, I think of her. I think of how, without any help from God or religion, she instilled in me an appreciation for simple goodness, for goodness' sake, and for no other reason. She had ample reason to be bitter, angry, disappointed, and frustrated, yet she was not. She was not a thoughtless woman, dully accepting life's lot because she did not know any better. She was sharp and clear about how she wanted to be in this world. She was uncomplaining by choice, saying, "What good would it do to complain?" when asked about her troubles.

Her mother—as I heard not from her, but from an aunt—was often inebriated, and quite possibly mentally unstable. She had a habit of showing up at school about midday and, with a ruckus, insisting that Florence, my grandmother, come home at once to take care of things. It must have been embarrassing to be called out by a drunk parent, one who when well oiled wore a cabbage leaf on her head in public for no apparent reason. If you asked my grandmother to talk about her mother, she would relate details, names, dates, facts, and events—but offer no analysis or condemnation.

That is why I felt so safe talking to her and baring my soul to her. There was no condemnation in her.

My grandmother chose goodness for no reason she would explain. She wanted no rewards and no recognition for choosing goodness. She expected no future eternal home in a gold-paved city for doing so. It was how she made things right in her world: by refraining from contributing anything that was not good. She would say, "Oh, for goodness' sake" at times when most people might say "goddam it!" I do not recall her cursing, other than once during a moment of extreme pain when arthritis in her knees, hands, and feet made it excruciating for her to stand. Once, in a moment of intense frustration, tears held back by force of will, she clenched her lips and muttered "dammit." I had never heard her say anything like it before. I looked up carefully from what I was doing to see out of the corner of my eyes if lightning would descend from whatever cruel god had set her up with such pain and suffering. She had endured so much and, through it all, had been so very, very good. If my grandmother could not make the grade and appease the spiteful gods, there was (as my mother would say) not a snowball's hope in hell for me.

When I caught my grandmother's eye, and she mine, she brushed my gaze aside with her gnarly fingers and looked away, but not in time to hide the tears. I knew better than to embarrass her by acknowledging them or looking at her while she wiped her cheek dry. I had learned from her that the best thing to do in a moment like this was to offer to make tea.

"How about a lovely cup of tea?"

She had made tea for me and so many others—grandchildren,

neighbors, and friends—when we had breakdowns, unwanted pregnancies, weaknesses, tragedies, coming-outs, and temper tantrums. She loved a good strong cup of tea and trusted it to do what nothing else could: to reestablish the goodness of things "once and for all," as she would firmly declare when passing sentence on trouble, or banishing a worry that one of us had poured out to her in sobbing detail.

I later learned that my grandmother had a much broader range of more risqué expletives, which she reserved for moments when her grandchildren were not around. But when she watched over us in the afternoons after school was let out, her language was care-filled, clean, and kind. We would test her, of course. We would try to distract her while she read one of the mysteries or romance novels in which she lost herself. I knew we were close to her limit when she would mutter "Why, you little . . ." and then stifle whatever word she had intended to use to complete the phrase. She would put on a show of being angry about almost saying the swallowed word, and would fuss and sputter and purse her lips, and then wrinkle them back into a smile.

My grandmother was good. She loved us unwaveringly, even when we were not good, like the way she loved her husband even when he didn't love her. Even when he hated her because he felt trapped in the large Catholic family. Even when he was violent, and blatantly unfaithful. Even through his extended periods of blind drunkenness and demeaning words said to her in public. She neither said a mean word about him nor encouraged anyone around her to do so. She sat by his side through his slow decline from cirrhosis of the liver. She tended to him with grace, much in the same way she tended to all who came to her in moments of distress: without a word of criticism, and with very little advice, but with careful attention and comfort—and, of course, with tea. Her love came through her listening, her tea, and her natural-born goodness. For this, friends and family came to her to sit, as in the presence of a wise teacher and pour out the contents of our troubled hearts.

Other than a supply of tea, novels, her rocking chair, and her grandchildren, she didn't need anything. She expressed no longing to accomplish great things or to see exotic places. She was quiet and took up little space in the world. She was enthusiastically grateful for the smallest of kindnesses extended her way. If you gave her something she did not want or like, you would never know because the fact that you gave her something in itself would be delightful to her.

She did not go to church. She was married in a church but would return only out of respect for a deceased relative, a wedding, or a baptism. She had no comment about religion or God, just as she had no comment about other people, her husband, or her pain. Goodness to her was something clear-cut, a decision. She believed in goodness, and in the rightness of things working out in the end, which was incredible to me, considering the rotten eggs life had thrown her way.

My grandmother was my hero and role model. She was always available to listen. I did not need to ask her if I could talk. Even if she was engrossed in a paperback novel, I could just start speaking. She would fold the book down into her lap on the apron that seemed a permanent part of her daily ensemble. She would listen attentively and would never criticize me. She was incapable of accepting that there could be anything wrong with me, and God knows I tried to persuade her. I told her about every transgression and crime of indulgence I was guilty of or was planning to commit. She would listen to me intently, but I couldn't make her agree with my self-damning conclusions. When I came apart one day, at sixteen years of age, in a howling mess at her tea table, confessing that I had become sexually active at too early an age, and that I had been slinking around pretending to be older than I was, drinking and smoking, and was brokenheartedly in love with a man twice my age, she couldn't be moved into shock or condemnation.

She set out at once to make the tea I didn't want, saying firmly, as she always did, "It'll all work out in the end," as she hobbled with painful steps to the kitchen and back with the assistance of countertops, chair backs, and other furniture to ease her way.

In severe cases, she would follow up, with annoying confidence, by adding the expression "There, there." If met with doubt, she would say, "Mark my words, it will all work out in the end," bringing the conversation to a full stop. It was both maddeningly simplistic and heartwarmingly satisfying to witness her conviction, which felt like medicine to whatever wound we brought to her.

She was right about so many things: about the power of choosing to be kind; about the inclination of things to work themselves out; about the futility of complaining, gossiping, or being mean-spirited; and about the pointlessness of contributing anything other than our natural-born goodness.

I did not know it then, but I do now: my grandmother's choices were shaping my character, and although I fail every day to be as resolute as she was, I owe my love of goodness, kindness, and compassion to her.

Florence May Panaino

Author's Note: About Meister Eckhart

Meister Eckhart, the medieval Christian mystic, wrote about spirituality in a way that reaches beyond a particular faith. He talked of a single component in people that he called the "soul" or "intellect," and thought of it as the foundation of humankind's potential for noble actions and good choices. He urged us not to flee from the world to discover this spiritual potential, but to find and embrace it wherever we are and in whatever we are doing. In the Penguin Classics publication *Meister Eckhart: Selected Writings* translated by Oliver Davies, Eckhart is described as one of the great speculative mystics of Western Europe who emphasized the importance of our spirituality not as something added to us, but as something that is permanently present, waiting for us to express. Whenever we turn to this light within us, he wrote, it will guide us to love goodness in ourselves and in others. Because of Eckhart's beautiful way of articulating the potential goodness within humankind, I've selected a quote of his to begin each section of *Ordinary Goodness.*

PART ONE
Ordinary Goodness

Spirituality is not to be learned by flight from the world, or by running away from things, or by turning solitary and going apart from the world. Rather, we must learn an inner solitude wherever or with whomsoever we may be. We must learn to penetrate things and find God there.*

—*Meister Eckhart*

---

* Matthew Fox, *Meditations with Meister Eckhart* (Rochester, VT: Bear and Company, 1983), 90.

The Paradox of Being

How Life Is a Paradox of Wholeness and Brokenness

Author Anne Lamott, on the eve of her sixty-first birthday, wrote a list of things she knows about being. The first on the list is that all truth is a paradox. "Life," she wrote, "is a precious unfathomably beautiful gift; and it is impossible here, on the incarnational side of things. It has been a very bad match for those of us who were born extremely sensitive. It is so hard and weird that we wonder if we are being punked. And it's filled with heartbreaking sweetness and beauty, floods and babies and acne and Mozart, all swirled together."* *Ordinary Goodness* is an invitation to look courageously into the unfathomable mystery of being—not as something to be solved, but as something to embrace and enjoy. Without this patient approach, it is tough to make sense of the ambiguities and contradictions that life is peppered with. To hold life gently, without insisting that it conform to predictable patterns and clear-cut

* Facebook post, April 8, 2015, https://www.facebook.com/AnneLamott/posts/662177577245222.

meaning, helps things flow a little more smoothly. A flexible view is essential when exploring goodness because it is inevitable that when studying goodness, we will encounter its opposite.

A friend told me the story of her visit to a Far Eastern spiritual teacher, a very sage and ancient man who spoke to her group for about forty minutes. When he had finished speaking, he opened the floor for questions, and one truth-seeker asked the sage for his thoughts about the state of the world, with all of its conflicts, crime, poverty, and war. The teacher sat in silence and considered the question, and then murmured shaking his head, "So sad, so sad." My friend said that it was as if she could see the world through his eyes for a brief moment.

I love the story of this sage and his utterance, "So sad, so sad." I do not feel the slightest bit discouraged by it. It helps me to know it is possible to see the world's conditions as they are, without losing sight of the natural goodness that is simultaneously present. The paradox of concurrently valid states that are opposite to each other fascinates me.

My friend's story reminded me of a poem by Ernest Holmes:

When death shall come
And the spirit, freed, shall mount the air,
And wander afar in that great no-where,
It shall go as it came,
Freed from sorrow, sin and shame;
And naked and bare, through the upper air
Shall go alone to that great no-where.
Hinder not its onward way,
Grieve not o'er its form of clay,
For the spirit, freed now from clod,
Shall go alone to meet its God.

I first encountered this poem at a time of grief and sadness. I liked it and felt comforted by the words, except that I struggled with the phrase "sorrow, sin and shame." I was in that phase of development where replacing every negative idea with something affirmative seemed necessary. I believed I had to reeducate my negatively habituated mind, and became inclined, for example, to replace the poetic words "wretch" with "soul" or "saint" in the hymn "Amazing Grace" because I could not tolerate the coexistence of wretchedness and goodness. Now I'm not so inclined to sugarcoat life. People like the sage, the poet, and the author of "Amazing Grace," John Newton, tell the story of humanity's journey through the valley of the shadows and are, I believe, at no time confused about the amazing grace available simultaneously while traveling through life's troubling territory.

Goodness is not necessarily sugarcoated. Ordinary goodness is both gritty and smooth, satisfying and frustrating, simple and confusing—and more.

It's Ordinary, and Natural

The idea of ordinary goodness came to me while teaching a class in which the students were learning the techniques of spiritual coaching. They questioned their ability to respond adequately to clients who were facing sorrow and tragedy. I asked them to settle down and think about a difficult time in their lives when someone did something for them that showed love. Some of them, teary-eyed, told stories about ordinary acts of kindness, while others told of gestures of compassion that went beyond the call of duty. The students either had a story of how loving-kindness from another person had touched them, or they identified with a story told by another student. I asked them if the giver of that love had any special skills. What was it that made the gift of love so meaningful? They answered that each giver had acted sincerely, from some natural instinct to care. I call that instinct ordinary goodness. I pointed out that they too had the same innate capacity to care, and that their goodness required no special training. It may be clumsy or unskilled, yet when expressed, especially through kindness, it leads to compassion. That is something mighty.

Practice
Notice Goodness and Share It

Donald Altman, in *The Mindfulness Code*, suggests that redirecting our attention to what we have in life does not cause us to ignore the real difficulties we, and those around us, may face. Rather, doing so helps us notice, appreciate, and enjoy the ordinary things that make life worthwhile. He provides this guidance:

> *First, turn your attention to what you have in your life from the very moment you wake in the morning. Appreciate the breath, the blankets that warm you, the shower that refreshes and cleans you, and even the alarm clock that wakes you up. Next, find a reminder of ordinary goodness that you can carry with you throughout the day, such as a picture of a loved one, a stone or other object from a memorable trip, or an inspirational quote. Finally, share your appreciation of ordinary goodness with others.**

On the seven-day, 545-mile AIDS/Lifecycle bicycle ride to raise funds for the San Francisco AIDS Foundation and the Los

---

* Donald Altman, *The Mindfulness Code: Keys for Overcoming Stress, Anxiety, Fear and Unhappiness* (Novato, CA: New World Library, 2010).

Angeles LGBT Foundation, there are many opportunities along the route to feel discouraged by exhaustion.* One longtime rider has paid attention to the plight of discouraged cyclists and, in response, created the tradition of leaving plastic eggs—the kind that are typically filled with candy at Easter—on cyclists' seats during the night. In the egg is a short note of appreciation and a reminder of the heroic nature of riding to help fund another person's well-being.

When I participated in the ride in 2015, some mornings my attention was not on ordinary goodness. I had no warm blanket to practice Donald Altman's exercise on, and the showers were crowded and cramped. I was focused on needing more sleep; I needed a break. I needed to quit, and I needed coffee. Then, when I found the egg on my bike seat, it had the marvelous and surprising effect of making me feel as enthusiastic as I did on day one of the ride. One quiet moment of redirecting my attention, facilitated by the kindness of a stranger, had the impact of changing my energy level, it seemed. More than that, it touched my emotional center, and I started to share encouragement with other struggling riders.

* AIDS/Lifecycle, www.aidslifecycle.org.

Goodness as Awe

How Caring About the Ordinary Things Causes Extraordinary Life Experiences

My grandmother's relentless willingness to be kind inspired me. She expressed kindness as if it were the most natural thing in the world. She took care to be interested in—even awed by—whatever was directly in front of her. She would exclaim "My goodness" and "Goodness gracious me!" frequently when reviewing a report card, a new hat, or a new friend one of us brought home. We felt the warmth of her caring because she paid attention to us. In that way, she invested time in us, making us think for a moment that we were amazing. We received her generous and focused interest, even when she was clearly in pain or would prefer to be left alone. She almost always gave her attention when it was called upon.

Not everything we did was awe-worthy. Nevertheless, she treated us as if we were truly wonderful. Surely, there must have been times when she was pretending to be interested. I could not tell if ever she was. Watching the ease with which my grandmother paid attention to others inspired me to try doing the same.

I practiced being interested in people in the same way that she showed interest in me. The more I tried, the easier it became. Not only that, but interest in others also turned out to be more enjoyable than I imagined it could be, and even felt genuine. I am a believer now in purposefully fostering the habit of being awe-filled and interested in life. It does not have to be the most colorful sunset to awe us. It does not have to be a gigantic sculpture or an exquisitely beautiful person or the biggest or most expensive something to stir us to awe. Awe and wonder are present in modest, ordinary things. When we accept awe and wonder to be an attitude of mind, with a little practice and creativity seeing the world with interest becomes a natural, and eventually permanent, addition to our worldview. It is precisely at times such as the ones we live in today that we must awaken the awareness of ordinary goodness by becoming attentive to and interested in it. We can start by becoming a little more interested in each other. You may doubt that it is possible to develop an interest in everyone, let alone have awe and wonder for them. You may question if it is natural to do so. But it can be done in the same way that we can learn other skills, such as writing. When I learned to write, I started, like everyone does, with the beginning exercise of mastering straight lines, which can be agonizing for some and easy for others. With patient encouragement from teachers and consistent practice, it came together, and I came to grips with the art of writing. Similarly, learning to type takes persistence. Remember the typing drills? We do not learn how to type by thinking about it. If we read a manual about typing, we might have some ideas about how to do it, but to *get it* into our fingers, we have to get into it. We have to invest time, and if we do so with a steady routine, we are rewarded with faster progress than if we approach it haphazardly. So it is with developing the awareness of ordinary goodness. We have to return steadfastly to the task and maintain slow, steady progress, which in itself is a challenge for a mind that is racing all the time.

Slow Down the Racing Mind

It is difficult for a fast-moving mind to connect with awe and wonder. It's hard to maintain interest in others and care about them when your mind is at the center of a storm of racing thoughts. Thoughts have to be slowed down for awe and caring to have a chance. When I pay attention to my thinking, I can see there is a difference in the speed of my thoughts when they are fearful, angry, selfish, or envious compared to when they are confident, loving, sharing, and kind. I perceive that when my mind is moving fast, it is prone to being unmindful. When I am paying attention to life or other people, the interest I show in them slows down my thinking to a gentle and mindful pace. Traveling at top speed in a vehicle makes the journey dangerous and raises the possibility of accidents. At high speeds, the landscape becomes a blur, and we cannot see details clearly, and that makes us prone to hurting others. It can be a challenge to enjoy a moment in nature, or with another person, when my thoughts are stacked one on top of the other and I am focused on something other than what or who is in front of me.

If I notice my mind speeding up, stimulated by fearful thoughts, I try to slow it down and bring it back to the present moment. I try to pay attention to whatever task is at hand as peacefully as I can. Sometimes I can spend a whole morning, or even a day, bringing my mind back to the present moment. When my thoughts move too quickly, I don't readily notice the experiences that have the potential to stop me in my tracks so that I say, "Oh, my goodness." We need those moments. They shine a light on our path, enlarge our perspective, and guide us through to the other side of our dark moments. These experiences of being stopped in our tracks from time to time expand our minds, and whether we say, "Goodness gracious me," or "Oh my God," or "Wow," these moments have the ability to unlock our untaught appreciation of what is good.

What is there to be awestruck by?

Consider the following questions and others like them as a way of slowing down the mind and practicing the feeling of awe and wonder: What did my neighborhood look like one hundred years ago? What will my community look like one hundred years from now? Or research the answers to questions such as: How far is it to the nearest star? How deep is the deepest ocean? Who were the indigenous people of the area I live in? What are the natural flowers in this area? What phase of the moon are we in? What was your great-, great-, great-grandmother's maiden name? What did her daily schedule look like? How do you know how to breathe, circulate blood, and digest food all at the same time? How do fingernails know how to grow, and how come you have the recipe to produce them while dealing with your problems at the same time? And, my goodness—do you realize that we are floating through space as living, breathing marvels, off somewhere on a tiny, precious blue ball and no one knows where it is or where it is going?

In Thornton Wilder's *Our Town*, Emily, a young girl who has died and looks back at her life, asks, "Does anybody realize how wonderful life really is while they live it?" I don't know if my grandmother had any regrets, but if she did, she kept them to herself—but not like hot coals burning dangerously in her pocket, filling her with pain and bitterness. She seemed present for the world around her. She seemed engaged and endlessly available to be amazed and interested in life. When she passed away, we sorted through her possessions. I was surprised to find, in her box of clearly most-treasured items, a rosary with a love letter from an officer of the United Kingdom's Royal Navy, along with his travel documents and a photograph dated from when she must have been sixteen years old, a few months before she was to be married.

We were speechless at the discovery. It seemed to point to a possible romantic tryst, and we marveled at the perfect silence with which she had hidden this skeleton in her cupboard all her life. Unfortunately, my mother, in her declining mental state, accidentally destroyed the contents of the box and many other photos and mementos of her own and my grandmother's life. I am so glad I slowed down to take in what we had found and cherish the memory I discovered among my grandmother's secrets. Since the loss of the material evidence of my grandmother's possible love affair, I try to slow down and treasure as many moments of life as I can.

Practice

Your Personal Commitment to Awe

Write a personal manifesto. For an example of a personal manifesto, see David Ault's "New Pledge of Allegiance" on page 157. Include in your manifesto several ideas you would like to commit to as a way of opening yourself up to the experience of awe for life. For example:

- I commit to praising and nurturing the talents and contributions of each person in my family or group.
- I commit to treating people as valuable and precious resources.
- I commit to resolving conflicts in gentle ways.

Create a steady routine of reading your manifesto. Read it first thing in the morning or as the last thing in the day. Post it somewhere where you will encounter it frequently and be reminded by it—for example, on your fridge door or on your bathroom mirror. Your personal manifesto can help refocus you on how you want to be in the world. Think of the manifesto as both a declaration of what is important to you as well as a statement of how you intend to live. Frequently reading your proclamation can serve as a compass, guiding you back to your essential goodness and reminding you about what is important to you and what is awe-inspiring in ordinary life.

Here are some questions you can ask yourself to help produce content for your manifesto:

- What, in life, is important to me?
- What would goodness have me do?
- What do I believe about the way life works?
- What inspires awe in me?

Let the answers to these questions form statements that inspire you. Make them short and easy to remember. If your manifesto becomes too long or too complicated, it may be difficult for it to take hold in your awareness and last throughout a day. Keep in mind that for the manifesto to be effective, it must focus on your desire to express what goodness would have you do in the world.

Avoid describing in your manifesto what is wrong with the world.

I Didn't Know What to Do

By five in the morning, I am all dressed up in my Air Force blues, checking every detail of the uniform, the shiny brass bits that the sergeant will examine first at inspection parade when I get to Air Force headquarters in Pretoria, South Africa. I am nineteen years old and grateful that I can commute rather than stay in the bleak, whites-only barracks in the capital, even though it means a lot of time spent on trains and in train stations neatly divided between black and white commuters. If I do not think about it too much, I can do what all the other white passengers are doing—not look at the overcrowded non-white platform. We do not see the people crowded onto a platform separated from ours by a mere invisible line, the crossing of which, I would learn, would invoke terrible consequences for those on both sides.

In my sleepy hometown suburb of Johannesburg, an hour's drive from the capital, the train station was old and stood open, exposed to the elements, with a bleak waiting room, wooden benches, a pay phone in a booth, and a ticket counter that seemed to me always to be deserted in those early hours when I waited for my train to Air Force headquarters. The small group of five or six whites stood politely far enough away from each other that "good morning" was not necessary. And there was that other platform, over there on the other side of the invisible barrier. On that platform, dozens of people crowded together in closeness that resulted in conversation, and noise and laughter and shouting, none of which I understood. We were not expected to understand them. They were expected to understand us, an expectation that would eventually result in riots when black Africans would finally say no to white oppression in South Africa's education system.*

Having caught the train so many times now, I knew what was coming without having to look. The screaming wheels of the train braking into the station would first bring the whites-only carriages, brightly lit, clean, and new, with a dozen or so passengers per carriage, followed by the non-whites carriages, stuffed beyond capacity with people. They sometimes hung out the forced-open automatically closing doors. The carriages would arrive at the station already full. The swell of people on the platform would nevertheless attempt to get on the train, to force their way into spaces between bodies. They had to get to work. The costs of not getting to work were terrible.

One day I sat comfortably in a whites-only train compartment. It was somewhat crowded, enough to cause the white folks to be particularly quiet. We seemed uncomfortable with the closeness. When the whistle from the conductor signaled readiness to depart

* On June 16, 1976, a series of student protests took place in Soweto, South Africa, against the introduction of Afrikaans as the main language of instruction in local schools. The protests, known as the Soweto Uprising, were met with brutal police force. The Afrikaans language was associated with the apartheid regime, and the decision to force education in Afrikaans was made without input from education professionals. The deputy minister of Bantu Education at the time, Punt Janson, said, "No, I have not consulted them and I am not going to consult them. I have consulted the Constitution of the Republic of South Africa." The Soweto Uprising marked the beginning of the violent collapse of the apartheid regime.

the station, the automatic doors began to creak closed, and the train began to move in jerky lunges, gathering momentum. Then as the doors made their final attempt toward closed position, a hand thrust itself between them, the hand of a late-arriving traveler who had nearly missed the train. He leaped forward, as was the custom, forcing the doors open even if it meant riding out of the station clinging to the already moving train. However, the hand was the wrong color. It was a black hand in a whites-only compartment, and the body that hurled itself awkwardly into the waiting area of the all-white compartment was a black man's body. Nobody looked directly at him as he composed himself and picked himself up in the wrong train compartment. And probably he was thinking right then about how to make his way back to the nonwhite compartment, but it was too late. He had crossed the invisible line. From nowhere, it seemed, police officers appeared. Smartly dressed, politely spoken, well-groomed keepers of order descended on him wielding batons. They beat him immediately, without question. He was on the wrong train. He was in the wrong compartment. He was the wrong color. It was all wrong. As long as we did not look, we could not see the police brutally beating him.

I didn't know what to do.

I felt my bottom lip quiver and bit it back. I knew what I had seen was wrong. I knew it was wrong. I stared at the passing landscape and let the sounds of protest and punishment dissolve into the background of the clickity-clack. I looked for my book to read. I did not look at anyone. As long as I didn't look I wouldn't see. My eyes were stinging; my cheeks were red with shame. Then I stole a look around at other passengers; only one looked back at me with a stern, wordless reprimand in his eyes.

"You know what happens to people like you, don't you?"

He was right. I had watched it happen countless times before.

I had also spoken up once when I was a preteen about race discrimination and learned it was not appropriate to do so. I remained anxiously quiet. Later, when the shame of not doing anything on the train had worked its way through me, I took a soul-searching look at what I had done by failing to act. I realized that indeed I did know what to do on that train. My grandmother and other role models had taught me exactly what my alternative actions might have been. The terrible shame I was feeling was precisely because I had not acted on what I knew. I lacked the courage to trust what ordinary goodness was inclined to do. I knew I had to refocus my life to embrace something more meaningful than my learned predisposition to self-preservation and personal safety.

I have struggled with the inclination to live from goodness because of how it has put me at odds with the instinct of self-preservation. I have struggled with speaking up for goodness when doing so would put me at odds with others and with the way everyone understood things to be. But when I have risked doing and saying what goodness would have me do and say, the results—while not always comfortable—have been satisfying in a soul-nourishing way. Similarly, whenever I turn away from goodness, the effect is that of feeling depleted. I have always wanted to trust that living from ordinary goodness would lead to a clearer understanding of how life works and that there would be rewards built into it. However, the journey has been different from what I expected. To pursue goodness is complicated, challenging, but at the same time rewarding.

More times than not the outcome of choosing the "more good" action or word has been unsatisfactory because it exposed me to the risk of being poorly treated, cheated, or vilified. Unexpectedly, though, my faith in ordinary goodness seemed not to depend on favorable outcomes but instead on integrity—I felt at peace with myself when I followed its prompting. I began to develop a difficult-to-substantiate, even unreasonable belief in goodness in general. I had to learn how to protect my confidence in goodness because there was little support for it from society in general. I had to look instead for support from the examples of ordinary people who were quietly going about their private business of living a meaningful life. In this regard, role models have been crucial in shaping and sustaining me.

What Would Goodness Do?

THE EVENT I experienced on the train marked a turning point in my life. It would lead, eventually, to my making a personal pledge to do as little harm as possible in the world, a commitment I would struggle to fulfill on a daily basis, regularly tripping over my unkindness and the tendency of my thoughts toward selfish choices. I searched for the answer to this question—what would goodness do in this or another situation? As I read the words of inspiring writers who wrote about the quest to live in balance with goodness, I sought words that would renew my commitment to try to live in a way that would make me proud. The poem "Desiderata," for example, by American writer Max Ehrmann, instructed me to go placidly through the noise and haste of the world and to remember that peace can be found in silence. Rudyard Kipling's poem "If" and Ecclesiastes 3:1–8 calmed me when the stress and challenges of life seemed overwhelming and reminded me that some things have enduring value and other things pass in time. More recently, I have been drawn to writings that are inclusive and lack condemnation. Sometimes they make their point boldly, as in the lyrics of Reverend Frederick Emerson Small's song "Everything Possible," which asserts the normalcy of diversity and affirms that no matter what you and I choose for our lives, or whom we choose to love, love will not be withheld from us.

These words helped and continue to help me form an idea of ordinary goodness as something that remains present during life's troubles, and to trust it, not undermine it, and not to give up when times are rough. Like the Twenty-third Psalm, especially in the gender-inclusive paraphrased version by Bobby McFerrin, which tells us that even though we may walk through a dark and dreary land, there is nothing that can shake us: She has said, She won't forsake us, that we are in Her hands.

Kahlil Gibran's words in *The Prophet* remind me that freedom comes not when we are finally without cares, but when we rise and break the chains that bind us despite the cares that girdle our lives. Og Mandino's *The God Memorandum* puts into words the secret that was whispered to us upon our birth—that we are each unique and miraculous—and has picked me up and set me back on my feet to face the world renewed many times (see the appendix section "Wisdom Writing Resources").

No matter how many times I immersed myself in elevating words or uplifting practices, I could not entirely shake the lingering knowledge that I *did* know what to do on that train where I witnessed the brutal beating. I had both my grandmother's modeling, and also the persistent reminder from my conscience. In my heart, I knew that what I had witnessed and the fact that I had chosen not to act were both wrong. I looked the other way because acting would intrude on my sense of personal safety. I began to realize that every time I stood on a segregated train platform, and every time I said nothing in the presence of injustice, my choices were whittling away some part of my integrity. On that train, and in other situations in my life—when events were not as brutal, but were equally lacking in decency—I had looked the other way and departed more and more from what I knew goodness would have done. And I did so for reasons ranging from as small as not wanting to feel uncomfortable to not wanting to cause conflict, to not wanting to be inconvenienced, and even to reasons, I regret to admit, such as not caring.

When I finally admitted to myself that on the train—and in other situations of injustice, cruelty, or even plain unkindness—I had knowingly chosen to look the other way, I experienced an awakening. The admission opened my understanding. I began to see that other choices are consistently available to me at such crossroads in life. Which path I chose depended on whether I would let goodness guide me. These options were available not only to me, I realized, but to anyone who would consult their goodness. For goodness to become a viable guide, I knew I had to break the habit of ignoring it. I had to pay attention to it, and when I did, I began to recognize that there are many possible paths to travel other than that of indifference to suffering. I started to see my ordinary life in a new light, with more ways to respond to the world. I started to see how fear and the need to fit in had in some cases fueled the choices I had made up until that moment. It was shocking to realize how much my culture had shaped me and taught me to act in a way that left me feeling empty. I discovered I had inherited a code of conduct that was ordinary, but not very good. The discovery was also exciting, in that I began to consider what my life might be like with a different code of conduct.

Conduct Code

Everyone has a code of conduct. It reveals itself in what we will do and what we will not do. Whether we come to that code unaware, absorbing it from our culture, or learn it from role models or inherit it from family members or choose it, it is there. It has less to do with what we think we should do, and more to do with our actions. For example, in moments like the one on the train when I failed to speak up, my personal code of conduct was showing itself. I had to break the pattern of ignoring goodness to selfishly protect my well-being. No matter what words I use to describe my character, my actions tell the true story of my conduct code. I might say that I cared about that man on the train, but my behavior told you I cared more about myself.

I overheard someone talk about her experience of being hosted by a local family instead of staying at a hotel when she was engaged to speak at an event in a small town. She said she was genuinely impressed by the kindness of the family and that she "knew them to be good, not by what they said but by what they did." Not only do I want to be known that way, but I also want my freedom to choose to be guided by respect for others. The personal choices we make to act, or not to act—as well as our strengths and weaknesses around food, alcohol, and everything else—may shape our characters, but they do not diminish the availability of goodness as an inner guide. For now, it is helpful to notice the degree of freedom there is to choose our actions and to begin seeing the related consequence of our choices. Freedom must be balanced with kindness, compassion, and respect for others. If it were not so, traffic intersections would be deadly crossings instead of organized streets with agreed-upon rules of conduct.

Fortunately, a code of conduct is not permanent. We can evolve it by interrupting patterns of behavior and paying attention to the promptings of goodness. It can change. All things may be possible, as Paul's first letter to the Corinthians states, but not all things are beneficial. This is a reminder that I can do, think, and speak in any way I like. Anyone can. Simply because something is possible does not necessarily mean that it is a good choice for building a life of meaning and worth. Simply because it is possible to cheat, gossip, use foul language, be mean-spirited, put my needs ahead of others', or use sarcasm and rudeness is not to say that behaving this way will take me where I want to go in life or make the kind of contribution to the world that I want to make as part of my legacy.

Before I considered the question "What would goodness want me to do?," I would rationalize my many questionable actions by pointing out that others were doing the same thing. If a person in authority bent a rule, I would make a mental check mark so that when I needed to justify something that was outside the boundaries of integrity, I could call upon that memory. I collected examples of wrongdoing to grant myself permission to do the same. None of this evidence helped me get past the fact that everyone has to pay their debts in life in the form of consequences for their actions. I have to be accountable for my actions, and you have to be for yours. I have to answer these questions without referring to the behavior of others: Am I happy with the way I have chosen to be in the world? Does my behavior in this life honor my original goodness?

With the contemporary social standard of "me first," we may have lost touch with the value of caring for others as much as we care about ourselves. When I place myself ahead of others in importance, there is less reason to respect others or to be kind to them. I do not mean to suggest that we should abandon developing healthy self-esteem. Neither do I propose that we stop caring deeply about ourselves or feeling pride for who we are and what we do. I do not mean to suggest that we should become doormats for others. But I am suggesting that if I think only of myself and the immediate gratification of my desires, I am going to make different decisions, quite different from ones I would make if I considered the well-being of others and the legacy that I'm going to leave behind by way of my code of conduct. When I remember that young people may be watching, I realize that my behavior is serving as a role model for the generations who will take ownership of the world. Rather than thinking of myself only, and rather than thinking of immediately gratifying a desire, and rather than persuading myself to do what feels good right now, I think more often about what goodness would have me do. Turning to goodness has guided me not necessarily into easier choices, but into choices that I can live with. With kindness as a compass, I learned to balance freedom with respect for others and discovered the joy of generously putting other people's needs in a place of higher importance than I had before.

Hooked on a Feeling

When I began exploring the answer to the question "What would goodness have me do?," I discovered how repeatedly my feelings influenced my choices. Fear, anger, jealousy, desire, love, and the like had a great stake in shaping my decisions. I allowed them to control my actions like powerful agents, with the authority to make choices on my behalf. More often than I like to admit, my conduct was being formed by feelings rather than by asking myself what was the right thing to do. Feelings are important gauges that point to what has heart and meaning for me. And even though they are excellent guides, I have come to question the maxim "Trust your feelings," and instead of blindly following my feelings, I have learned to trust goodness to be the more reliable guide. For example, my feelings might focus my attention on self-satisfying choices, whereas when I asked myself "What would goodness have me do?," the question frequently prompted me to look beyond immediately satisfying my feelings and helped me think of how my choices affected others.

Becoming unhooked from the urges of a self-satisfying feeling may be a formidable task, but it is possible. I understand the metaphor of a tempting devil better now that I have attempted to resist feelings that seem to want me to make unhealthy choices. I could easily blame the devil when I was younger because it was convenient to do so when I did not wish to take responsibility for my actions . . . actions I knew were less than decent or that were self-destructive or uncharitable.

My grandmother was relentless about taking responsibility for her actions. She had a curious expression that she used on us when we claimed someone made us do something against our better judgment. She would say, "Oh, my foot, *you* did it without any help from anyone else." I don't know why invoking her foot had such a high impact, but when we heard the phrase, we knew we would have to own up and take responsibility for our actions. It instilled in me the idea that no one can remove themselves from responsibility for their choices. I didn't like hearing it then, and I tried to ignore it in my young adult years. Now, I understand it better. Owning what I have done helps me understand who I am. I see that my choices are my ethics in action; no matter what picture I paint of my personality, the real me comes across through my choices and actions. Now I know that I can say all the beautiful things I want about how I think I ought to behave, but if I get up and act in a way that contradicts those words, my actions will make the stronger statement. My actions reveal my character more clearly than my words ever will.

Integrity

Integrity, among other things, means the condition of symmetry between words and actions. And that, it seems, requires ongoing attention to sustain. Once, on a visit to the island of Catalina off the coast of Los Angeles, I had the opportunity to witness how easy it is for me to say one thing and then behave in a different way. I had been trying to take responsibility for my actions by acting with integrity. For example, if I said honesty was important, my goal was to be honest. If I said kindness was a value of mine, I attempted to weed out unkind actions. But, instead of focusing on myself, I got sidetracked by lapses of integrity in other people, ready to pounce on their slightest infraction. My communications skills were still unrefined by the study of nonviolent communication, and I had not learned the art of speaking mindfully. I sometimes acted in the way new converts to a diet or newly converted nonsmokers occasionally do: I overstated my point of view—and, in my case, with unkind words—and I insisted other people master the integrity, or kindness, or honesty that I was aiming to accomplish. No matter that I was not yet able to embody these qualities; I still insisted that other people comply with them.

I was waiting on the pier for the ferry to return day visitors back from Catalina to the California mainland. Before me was a little slice of paradise. There they were, all those coral-loving fish in the beautiful, clear water, close enough to the surface to be seen. The scene, one that could be featured in *National Geographic*, was magnificent. Then I spotted a potential offender: a man, leaning on the same railing, smoking. In my mind, I imagined how the scene would play out, and he obliged. He approached the end of his smoke, and as I had predicted, he threw the still smoking butt into the ocean. My mind flipped back and forth between intruding on someone else's life and advocating for nature. I was ready to let an outraged and indignant response burst out in a loud voice. "Hey, you, what do you think you're doing?" I was going to say. I rehearsed my reprimand in my mind for a few seconds before speaking. I hesitated because I understood that an already problematic situation was possibly going to get even worse when I acted out of integrity with my stated claim that I was a kindhearted person. I felt pressure to come up with something to say that was kind and also addressed the perceived wrongdoing. I did not want to avoid my responsibility, and I did not wish to act out of integrity with my newfound value of kindness. I took another microsecond to examine if my planned response matched how I wanted people to know me in the world. I asked myself what might be the most beautiful way to address what had happened. My preference to disturb no one was butting up against my inclination to take a stand for the environment. I took yet another microsecond to think of the dramatic and powerful illustration when Jesus met with the people at the city gates, where they were about to stone to death the woman who had committed adultery. He said to them, "Let the one among you without sin cast the first stone." I refer to this piece of wisdom frequently to temper my indignation—not to relieve me of the obligation to speak, but to prompt me to consider situations in which I act the same way as those I am accusing. In this way, my activism is enhanced because I get to see myself as part of the situation and not apart from it. This softening of my perspective doesn't weaken my position; rather it opens doors to conversations that are closed when using a more accusing approach. But that day, the Jesus story wasn't soothing my ire. I was feeling outraged, and my outrage was guiding me to scold the litterbug harshly.

This deep internal process I was in lasted mere seconds, and while I was in it, somebody else next to the man leaned over and, with a smile, whispered to the butt-flinging tourist, "Oh, the fish can't eat that; it's harmful to them." Because there was something genuinely kind in his smile, the comment seemed more like a private conspiracy between friends than like a stern reprimand. Had I not been standing so close I might have missed the private exchange. The smoker nodded sheepishly, looked around to see who had heard the words, and mumbled, "You're right." The kindly rebuker probably achieved much more than I ever would have, if I had let my anger and frustration flare up and cast the first stone. I try to remember, when I am frightened, indignant, or self-righteous, to act in the name of goodness, like Malala Yousafzai. Her voice for education in the midst of death threats and unjust sanctions in Pakistan against girls' education placed her on *Time* magazine's 2013 list of The 100 Most Influential People in the World, and she speaks with a clear, calm, non-accusing, and forgiving tone to deliver her message.* Many would say she would be justified if she were to be furious, outraged, or vengeful. But her message carries the weight it does, in my opinion, because of its clarity and gentleness, more than it would were she to succumb to hatred.

Ever since considering the questions "What is right?" and "What is wrong?" and "What would goodness do?," it seems that I cannot escape my duty to speak up, and to do so as kindly as possible. Goodness urges me to pay attention to people, to intuition, to the minority opinion, and to marginalized voices. The more I follow its calls, the more I see others in the world performing acts of kindness, choosing the higher road, and putting others before self. Goodness has started to become fascinating because I am interrupting habits that prevent me from following its guidance, and I'm mindfully searching out evidence of its presence in the world.

Practice
How to Change Other People

A manager of a small bookstore told me a humorous story about a book in her store that would sell very well. Because the title was so attractive to people who were interested in changing other people, customers would pick it up eager to learn the secret of how to

* "The 2013 Time 100," *Time*, April 18, 2013.

change the negative people in their lives. The book *How to Change Other People* by Raymond Charles Barker turned out to be a great disappointment to many of those who purchased it because ultimately the book was more about how to change themselves rather than changing other people.

Nevertheless, for anyone who would like to learn the secret of changing negative people, that is entirely the secret—the change takes place within *you*. This kind of change is magical in its effect, and it's well worth the effort to try to learn how to do it. You might even think of it playfully as learning to cast happy spells on negative people. It can be fun and useful as long as you keep this secret in mind: you are not doing anything to anyone other than to yourself. Until you can remove the label of "negative" from the person with whom you are dealing, and until you can be willing to be the person to change first, you will probably not have the hoped-for results.

Getting Started

Begin by choosing the person you want to practice on. You might not wish to start with the most challenging candidate right away. Start with someone who you think is negative and who represents a low-level irritation, and set your sights on changing them by changing yourself. Preferably, start with someone with whom you have frequent contact so that you can easily monitor the effectiveness of your life-changing program. For this exercise to be truly effective, you ought to have a notebook that you can set aside for this task. Give yourself time to write down your honest assessment of this person's negativity. This is no time to hold back. Write down every thought that comes up—after all, you are not going to be sharing these thoughts with anyone, and you are certainly not going to be expressing them to your candidate. What you will be doing with this exercise, however, is allowing yourself to express what is inside you. This is a powerful first step in getting started with the change process. Think of it as healthy venting. Once your opinion of the person has been expressed in writing, it has the effect of relieving the pressure of holding these thoughts inside. Now that they are on paper, you can take a sigh of relief and prepare yourself for step two.

What's in the Mirror

This next step is where most practitioners of the art of changing other people will fail; their inability to assess themselves with the same bluntness and honesty that they use to evaluate their offender is what ultimately undoes them. It takes a tremendous amount of courage and humility to answer this question: Where am I like that too? The way you use the question is to go over what you wrote down about the person you wish to change, sentence by sentence, pausing after each one to ask yourself, "Where am I like that too?" Do this calmly, serenely, and blamelessly. It is not about finding ways to make yourself wrong; rather, it's about softening the mental grip we have on where other people fall short of our standards.

Next Steps

What is next? you might ask. This is the beauty of the exercise. Nothing is next. You go about your life as you normally would and notice the subtle changes that take place in you when you think about that person or talk to them. Most importantly, be gentle with yourself and try to have fun noticing how very much we all are alike. The fourth item on Anne Lamott's list of things she knows is this: "Everyone is screwed up, broken, clingy, and scared, even the people who seem to have it more or less together. They are much more like you than you would believe. So try not to compare your insides to their outsides. Also, you can't save, fix or rescue any of them, or get any of them sober. But radical self-care is quantum, and radiates out into the atmosphere, like a little fresh air. It is a tremendous gift to the world. When people respond by saying, 'Well, isn't she full of herself,' smile obliquely, like Mona Lisa, and make both of you a beautiful cup of tea."*

* Facebook post, April 8, 2015, https://www.facebook.com/AnneLamott/posts/662177577245222.

Goodness as Altruism

Ordinary Goodness Is Helping People in Need

In South Africa, the parable of the Good Samaritan is one of the stories we frequently heard in school at a time when Bible studies and school prayer were mandatory. Jewish children had permission to skip Bible studies because our lessons were almost exclusively based on New Testament stories. I watched them longingly as they exited from what was becoming the most unbearable part of school: mandatory listening to implausible stories told by teachers who permitted no questions and no discussion. Now and then, despite my disdain, I would find myself engaged in a story, like the one about the Good Samaritan, a traveler whose ethnic identity stereotypes him as the least likely to stop and help a traveler who has been robbed, beaten, and left for dead. Before the Samaritan pauses to assist the battered traveler, others have not stopped who might have been expected to be more likely to do so. Jesus told the story in response to a question about what Leviticus 19:18 meant: "Do not seek revenge or bear a grudge against anyone among your people, but love your neighbor as yourself."

I don't know if my grandmother ever heard the story of the

Good Samaritan, but I do know that she never turned anyone away who needed help. In the South Africa of my childhood, the separation between whites and blacks extended to everything. Even offering help to those in distress was divided by race. If a person's skin was of a different color, the view was that help could justifiably be withheld. But my grandmother was color-blind in that regard and would apply the same "cup of tea" remedy to anyone—no matter their race, religion, or gender. Thinking of her, and the Samaritan, I am reminded again that actions speak louder than words. I am reminded to keep fresh before me the values I aspire to live by so that they will be apparent to an observer.

What is a value? It is a principle or quality considered worthwhile or desirable—a guiding standard. What do you stand for? What guides you in your life? There can be a gap, or difference, between actual values that guide my life and values I think I should have. The gap shows up in the difference between what I talk about as important in my life and how I actually live my life. My years of working in the movie market-research industry in Hollywood showed me that people will say they do not like a movie if they think they are supposed to dislike it. If they believe saying no to a movie reflects the correct value, they will say no. However, they can be counted on to go and see the movie nevertheless, as long as it is exciting and has the right combination of elements that entertain them. Even if the content of the movie flies in the face of their statement of disapproval, they will pay to see it.

The story of the Good Samaritan makes me think of a value I talk about and aspire to live by—altruism. Altruism and compassion each has its beauty. The beauty of compassion grows out of a perceived shared experience, when we *feel* along with those who suffer. That is the "com" in compassion . . . *with* others, an awareness of the pain and suffering of others often coupled with the desire to relieve it. Compassion arises when we have an awareness of our pain and, from that identification, are moved to want to alleviate the suffering of others.

The beauty of altruism is slightly different, in that it grows out of a personal desire to express certain qualities like goodness, compassion, and kindness, whether or not there is a trigger event or tragedy or perceived need. It is a purposefully chosen expression of goodness and kindness regardless of whether suffering is present. In that way, then, altruism is not necessarily a response to human distress, although it can be and often is. But what makes altruism different is that it is driven by a desire to connect and contribute. Sometimes it may be based on a personal awareness of how wonderful it is to be helped, assisted, or valued. The Random Acts of Kindness movement that has spread across the world like wildfire—bringing to widespread awareness the practice of paying for the car behind you on a toll bridge, for example—is a movement of altruism. Altruism grows out of the belief that it is good and right to help and to contribute to the lives of others.

We come alive when we express that kind of goodness; it fills us with satisfaction. In the New Living Translation of the Bible, Matthew 5:45 is rendered as ". . . and he sends rain on the just and the unjust alike," reminding me that altruism in its highest form, like the actions of the Good Samaritan, need not be reserved for those in my intimate circles. It is rather a general attitude toward life and does not require people to be deserving of the good extended to them. Another quality that defines altruism is that it does not expect anything in return. It does not require recognition or thanks. It does not require the recipient to be worthy of the act. It is a function of the natural inclination to goodness of the one acting altruistically.

There is a struggle inside of me between my desire for recognition and the desire to act altruistically. To balance the desire for recognition, I sometimes play a game by paying for someone's dinner in a restaurant where I am eating, but without disclosing that it was me who paid for their dinner. I try to leave the restaurant before the unsuspecting guests receive their "paid in full" receipt. I find the experience especially satisfying when I have no idea how it was received.

Altruism is expressed as not only physical acts of kindness but as an attitude of mind. My favorite expression of this attitude of mind was written by Hugh Prather in *The Quiet Answer*:

> *Who really knows the effect of one happy thought? Is it possible that it circles the globe, finding entry into any open heart, encouraging and giving hope in some unseen way? I am convinced it does. For whenever I am truly loving, I feel the warmth and the presence of the like-minded, a growing family whose strength lies in their gentleness and whose message is in their treatment of others.**

A quality that comes to mind when I think of altruism is that of spontaneity—or, rather, not waiting for circumstances to be optimal before acting. Altruism doesn't require perfect conditions. It can burst into being, sometimes without warning, as illustrated by this entry submitted to the Random Acts of Kindness organization's website, titled "Just a Little Thing":

> *During the rush and bustle of the Christmas holiday, I slipped into the local coffee shop drive-through. My paycheck was pretty much spent, and my kids and I still had grocery shopping to do. In the rear view mirror, I noticed a pickup truck with a father and small son. Impulsively, when at the window paying*

---

* Hugh Prather, *The Quiet Answer* (New York: Doubleday, 1982).

*for my bill, I also asked to pay the bill for the truck behind me. My kids asked why, and I explained about how doing a kind thing was really more for me than for the receiver, though I hoped he enjoyed it. My kids wondered as to my timing, as we were off to the bank to see our balance before hitting the grocery store. Much to my surprise, there was more money than expected. We had overpaid on mortgage/taxes through the year, and the bank had deposited the surcharge back into our account just that morning. Coincidence? Maybe, but I can't help thinking that when you share of yourself, you always get back so much more.**

Wayne Muller, the founder of the organization Bread for the Journey,† delivered a keynote address at a convention in California that I attended. In his presentation, he talked about how some people wait to perfect their contribution before they give it. They delay making a contribution to the world because they doubt that the world's suffering can be stopped in a meaningful way by their participation. We sometimes question ourselves when the urge to share arises, and we pull back, second-guessing the urge to contribute, like Moses did when he received the call to lead his nation to safety, asking "Why me?" I can't do this—I'm no good at it. The idea that "you must first learn to love yourself before you can love someone else" comes to mind. It is an idea that became popular during the New Age movement. I now doubt the accuracy of the opinion, and I tend to think that you and I as we are, with all our imperfections, have a valid and wanted contribution to make to the world. In other words, you and I can care about and support each other long before we have perfected self-love. Postponing the

---

* The Random Acts of Kindness Foundation, www.randomactsofkindness.org.
† Bread for the Journey, www.breadforthejourney.org.

expression of loving-kindness until we have mastered self-love may be a terrible idea.

The way Wayne Muller started his organization, as I remember the story, was by putting aside a portion of his therapy fees and using them to fund acts of altruism—not necessarily big operations, but small local enterprises that served the community. Whether that was a local group helping people to learn crafts or students installing sustainable gardens, he started this project because he felt he had something to offer. He might not have known what it was exactly or what form it would take, but he didn't let his lack of knowing stop him. He started putting aside funds a little at a time until he had enough to help one project. Many Bread for the Journey projects were started by ordinary people who want to contribute to life. For example, Project Restoration was founded by a minister who believed that every child has vast potential and that the difference between success and failure frequently comes from the care and support of the community. So he got a small grant from Bread for the Journey to purchase equipment to train ten- to seventeen-year-olds in basic computer skills. Another example is that of a teacher helping students to train abandoned dogs to be service animals. What inspires me about these projects is that even though they cannot relieve the suffering of the entire world, they are nevertheless contributing something to the world for goodness' sake. Someone had an idea, and with it a sense of excitement and possibility. Jana Stanfield in her song "All the Good" reminds us that we cannot do all the good that the world needs, but the world needs all the good that we can do.

How can you bring altruism alive in your life? You don't have to come up with an idea for a project, although that is great too—you can begin practicing immediately with the simplest form of altruism, common courtesy. Letting others go first, saying please and thank you, and being nice. I know that the word *nice* is a trigger for some people and evokes images of disingenuous communication. I question whether being authentic and real can turn out to be anything but kind and generous. Consider these synonyms related to nice: friendly, generous, warmhearted, understanding; charitable, humane; considerate, forbearing; tolerant, agreeable; beneficial. That is what being "nice" means.

I have asked myself on occasion, what would change in my life if I were to focus on any one of these qualities for a day? I have tried it, and the results are wonderfully rewarding. I do not always stick to the practice for an entire day, but during the time I do focus on one of these qualities, the effect is pleasing. Once when I moved into a neighborhood, my new neighbor brought me a plate of homemade cookies as a welcome gift. I had not yet slowed down during the business of moving to notice even that there were other living beings on either side of the house. It was a very nice thing to do. The random act of kindness influenced me to slow down and be more present. Later when I moved again to another neighborhood, no one brought me cookies, and it occurred to me that it was my turn. So I started making an effort. I made a point of greeting and talking to the elderly man who walked his dog every day past my house, and to smile and catch the eye of people leaving for their work commute at the same time as I did.

Practice

Slow Down and Notice

In *Beyond Courage: The 9 Principles of Heroism*, Chris Benguhe writes in the chapter on altruism that we have to slow down to be able to notice and get to know the people around us. It is difficult to get to know people when we are moving quickly through the world:

> *We need to take the time to see our friends, family, neighbors, colleagues, and even people on the streets as human beings who possess all the same emotions, concerns, fears, and loves that we do. Once we accomplish that, we can communicate and bond with them through those commonalities. Eventually, the barriers of fear, hatred, and hurtfulness will dissipate and be replaced with our common goal of happiness. Again, I stress we must make the time to do this every day in our hustle and bustle lives, not just occasionally when it is convenient to do so.**

Think about the people in your neighborhood, or in your work environment or wider circle of friends. It is possible you know personal details about the people in your close circles, but what about people at the office? Do you know when their birthdays are, or what their favorite foods are, or where they like to vacation? Experiment with ways to slow down and notice the people around you, by taking the time to inquire about these simple questions in a non-invasive way. Being gently curious about other people can help you slow down and take in more information about them.

* Chris Benguhe, *Beyond Courage: The 9 Principles of Heroism* (New York: Perigee, 2003), 124.

When Goodness Is Not Enough

How to Trust Goodness in the Face of Life's Tragedies

When the Amish community of Lancaster County, Pennsylvania, sent their children to school one morning in 2006, I'm confident that they hoped for nothing less than the best for their children. I'm confident they had no idea that the dreadful day would end with mourning their children, murdered by the hand of a gunman. For even the most avid believer in ordinary goodness, this event—and others like it—poses a deep and challenging question: How can any of this be good? Personally, I wouldn't dare try to explain this situation in terms of an all-pervading goodness. I wouldn't be foolish enough to suggest to the parents of the slain children that they seek a silver lining. If anything, goodness, if listened to, prompts me in situations like these to be still with humility at the utterly unfathomable complexity of life and the fragile nature of existing as a human being. I would offer only my love and support. The goodness I find in situations like these is in the way people love and support each other, not in the event itself.

I was traumatized by the news of the event, as much of the country was at the time. I wondered what to make of it. It occurred to me that one of the most difficult times to find understanding is while a crisis is unfolding. Yet it is the exact time when we most need and want to search for the answer to the question "Why?" Sometimes it is necessary for many years to pass so that the long look back across time can reveal what hidden insight might come from an experience of tragedy. Even so, naming a tragedy good at all seems to be a disservice to the people involved, whose lives were permanently impacted. Who can look at the Holocaust, apartheid, slavery, war, forced assimilation of Native Americans, or torture and call any part of it good? Instead, these humanity-shaping events leave us with, if anything, what I prefer to call a dark gift. Sometimes that gift is in the form of the wisdom to never allow such an event to happen again, or sometimes it is in the form of increased appreciation for our tenderness and vulnerability. Sometimes the dark gift comes as a reaffirmation of the fragile nature of life.

I am grateful to the Amish community for leading the country through that tragedy in a way that reignites my faith in goodness. In a letter in *Chron*, David Capes of Houston wrote:

> *But before their innocent children were cold, the Amish community was giving us all a lesson in forgiveness by gathering in small groups to pray for the grace to forgive [gunman] Roberts and to pray for his family. By the end of the day, some even said they had forgiven him and asked the nation to turn their prayers to Roberts' wife and children. The Amish are an amazing people, characterized by a simplicity and radical obedience to the gospel, even the part about forgiving your enemies. We don't know why Roberts attacked the school girls and then killed*

> *himself, but the inability to forgive himself and God seems to have led to a horrible evil.**

Later in the letter, Capes writes something that struck me deeply and has stayed with me. The Amish people didn't arrive at this incredible ability to forgive their children's murderer on that one day alone. They got there after many years of practicing their faith. Forgiveness is one of the cornerstones of the Amish way. It made me think about the cornerstone practices of my life. What would I describe as a cornerstone of my conviction? I don't know anyone whose life has not been touched by tragedy, or loss, or disappointment in some profound way. My family, although relatively privileged in the scheme of things, has had its share of shocking news. My seventy-something-year-old uncle and his wife were murdered in their home in January 2004 by robbers looking for cash. I had been waiting for this lesson from the Amish and their cornerstone conviction to be able to say my first words of forgiveness toward the murderers of my family.

I have been thinking too about a time when my brother fell. He was epileptic, prone to having seizures, and was developmentally challenged. We were fortunate enough to be able to take care of him ourselves for most of his life. However, it meant paying constant attention to him to guard against accidents as a result of the occasional seizures. They weren't violent; he would gently phase out of consciousness. The real difficulty was that he would fall. One day when he had one of those falls, I was far away enough that I couldn't prevent the descent. He fell onto a sharp-cornered wall, which made a deep gash in his head.

Now, I'm not fond of blood. Not even two years in the Air Force

---

* Letters: "Lessons of Amish Tragedy," October 7, 2006, *Chron*, http://www.chron.com/opinion/outlook/article/Letters-Lessons-of-Amish-tragedy-1903388.php.

and volunteering for end-of-life service organizations made me any more resilient. I get queasy at the thought of blood and am likely to fall over myself. But something wonderful happened to me that day of my brother's fall, something that I could only call *wonderful* many, many years later. Today, when I think back to it, I remember it as a feeling of time being suspended, or of everything being in its right place. For want of a better term, I would say it's what I think about when I hear the phrase "a holy moment." It was, I imagined, what the eye of a storm must be like. I cherish that moment in time and wouldn't trade the experience for anything, even though it involved blood. What happened was that something in me put aside all my fears, dislikes, and preferences and prompted me to walk over to where my brother had fallen. I placed my hand on the wound at the back of his head to stop the profuse bleeding as if it was the most ordinary and logical thing to do—as if I had been trained to know what to do.

There is an old hymn made popular again by Enya, the words of which announce, "What tho' the tempest 'round me roars, I hear the truth it liveth."* I sometimes cannot see ordinary goodness because I'm looking at the storm, thinking that I have to quiet the wind and still the waters before I can ask the question "What would goodness have me do in this situation?" I wonder now if that is a reasonable point of view. Storms are everywhere and constantly rising and dissipating. Should I hold myself responsible for helping the whole world and everything in it when I cannot take credit for knowing how to breathe, assimilate oxygen, digest food, make tears, or perform any number of other physiological wonders that continue to be available even when my attention fixes on a current storm? Sometimes I think that it is all up to me, that if my faith is strong enough or my plan clear enough, or my commitment pure enough or my prayers convincing enough, then surely I will get to

* Robert Wadsworth Lowry, "My Life Flows on in Endless Song."

the other side of whatever ails me. In reality, even people of immense faith and immense goodness face tragedy. That's life. And goodness doesn't wait for storms to be quiet. Goodness is about how I walk through the storms of my life. When difficulties arise, sometimes I panic, but now I have learned to pay attention and notice the moments when panic appears to see if I can interrupt the inclination and return my attention to something calming and empowering.

In the case of my brother's fall, I didn't have the time to contemplate peace or conduct a calming mindfulness exercise. But there was goodness in me in the form of love, and it rose up to prompt me to engage in the task at hand. I would say that I did not arrive at the strength to do that in one single day of loving my brother. It came from years and years of the challenge of living with and caring for him while attempting to stay in a loving frame of mind and handle the many less-than-perfect situations that his condition produced for our family. The love took me beyond my ordinary fear. If someone had told me during those painful years of caring for my brother that his illness and falls were a gift, or if they had prompted me to look for the silver lining, I would have thought that person to be idiotic and out of touch with the challenges our family was enduring. Now, years and years later, as I look back, I see it from a different perspective—and I see how much of who I am has been molded by his presence in my life. Now I do see it as a gift that shaped my life for the good.

I've had the privilege in my career to speak to many people who find themselves in a life-storm. Many have expressed to me that they don't feel like they can make it to the other side of tomorrow. Some tell me that they feel overwhelmed by the circumstances and think that they lack preparation, understanding, and sometimes the physical strength to get through what they are facing. They don't feel equipped to complete the journey, and many have said they would be grateful for a moment's peace. I don't always know how to advise them, other than to share what I do to help myself to stay the distance during times of stress and challenge. One of the methods I use is to read something that will redirect my thinking and calm me. Although I am not a Christian or a Jew, I have found some comfort in reading some of the prayers from those faith traditions, such as Psalm 139 in the King James Version of the Bible:

Whither shall I go from thy spirit?
Or whither shall I flee from thy presence?
If I ascend up into heaven, thou art there;
If I make my bed in hell, behold, thou art there.
If I take the wings of the morning, and dwell in the uttermost parts of the sea,
Even there shall thy hand lead me,
And thy right hand shall hold me.
If I say, Surely the darkness shall cover me,
Even the night shall be light about me.
Yea, the darkness hideth not from thee,
But the night shineth as the day;
The darkness and the light are both alike to thee.

The Satsang teacher Gangaji writes about a similar method of pausing to let mental activity stop and to let your mind become available for what it does not yet know. The idea is to create an opening of silence for your true Self. "Reflection," she writes, "means to give up all considerations, all computations, all measurements, and just be still."* I love that. I love it because it helps me to remember, in times of challenge—when my mind demands explanation, when I think I'm not enough for the task before me—to trust the natural rising of wisdom and insight that have

* Gangaji, *You Are That* (Boulder, CO: Sounds True, 2007).

been accumulating in me for years, establishing in me a cornerstone conviction that goodness remains present always, and to make room for the reflective inner quietness that grants access to that conviction, rather than letting my mind fester with anxious thoughts.

When I can successfully interrupt my mind, whether by reading something or simply noticing what is happening, I inevitably discover that peace has always been present and available in me. Like goodness, it doesn't need to be created—it exists. It doesn't have to be conjured by prayers—it is already there. It exists naturally in us as our goodness and can be consulted in moments of focused quietness to guide us through life's difficulties.

Practice

What Are Your Values?

How do you decide between what is right and what is wrong? Having clarity about your own values will help you to be clear about when you are not keeping them. An interesting exercise is to imagine what someone memorializing you will say about you. Imagine the speaker at your memorial saying, "[Your name] was the living example of ______________________________. You could always count on her/him to ____________________________ ____________. It was clear by what he/she did that he/she valued ______________________________."

If you are uncertain about how to complete these sentences, try asking close friends how they would complete them about you. What, in their opinion, are your values? How they respond may not match your own sense of your personal values, but it may give you an idea of how other people experience you. It may help you understand how the way you are showing up tells the world what you stand for.

Goodness as Love and Devotion

Devotion, a Practice That Reconnects Us to Our Ordinary Goodness

Devotion is ardent—and often selfless—love. Devotion can be focused inwardly on an idea or principle, or outwardly on a person or project. It is a unique expression of love characterized by reverential attention. Devotion seeks no recognition and is satisfied in itself—it is given without need for reciprocation. In some faiths, regular or daily devotion is encouraged through acts of worship, or deeds of compassionate service to others, or sometimes through expressions of art. Whatever the form, the idea is that through these activities individuals may encounter something larger than themselves or, in religious terms, the Divine—symbolized in the object of the service.

Devotion can be practiced anywhere. It can be practiced at home during private mindfulness practices—such as meditation, in which a person contemplates a favorite writing or scripture (see the appendix for "Wisdom Writing Resources" suitable for this method). It can be practiced in a formal, sacred ceremony at a place of worship—such as during a mass when a devotee focuses reverentially on the symbol of the holy host. Or it can be practiced simply by being in the presence of someone who, because of their spiritual practice, radiates an air of inward peace. It can be experienced at work by mindful attention to whatever task is being done, or by tending to a grandchild, parent, or sick animal. At the heart of this focused care and attention is generosity of spirit: the best attention and energy available at the moment is given to the task or person. It is often the case that when serving another in this way, no resentment or resistance is present, but rather a feeling of love arises—and helping another becomes more compelling than whatever else may be on the calendar.

There is an even deeper place from which to express devotion: the recognition of our connectedness to each other. Some of the great spiritual traditions describe Divinity as a unifying life force that connects all of creation, imparting a spark of itself into all that it created. For those who believe this way, everyone and everything are potential objects of reverential loving-kindness. In some forms of the Hindu faith, devotion to the Divine in all of creation is called *bhakti*, and it is thought by some to be the most fundamental, and most accessible, of all spiritual practices—because love, like goodness, is natural to all. Practicing love on this basis of connectedness is potentially the end of all suffering.

Our modern culture defines happiness in terms of success and having whatever we want. It takes steadfastness not to succumb to the constant message that everything of worth is external. There is nothing wrong with enjoying the things of this world, nothing wrong with enjoying personalities and people and their antics, nothing wrong with taking care of the comforts of these creatures that our human bodies are. I like to celebrate all of this life because it is all part of the superb production called creation. My challenge is not to let it become the sole object of my attention. This culture makes that a real challenge by insisting with fervor that everything that is temporary is important. It pleads with us to possess things before it is too late, before time runs out, before the price goes up, before we are too old, urging us to buy whatever is being advertised—and to own, keep, and protect it. We are invited to become devoted to that which lacks substance and cannot satisfy our longing for a life of depth and meaning.

Some relief comes in the form of seeing things for what they are—beautiful effects of creation—and, instead of adoring them, cherishing the source from which they came. For now, it is important not to confuse devotion with other energy-depleting activities in which a person gives his time or dignity away to atone for a wrongdoing or to attain another's approval. Neither is it an act of devotion if your attention to someone is unwanted or leaves them feeling drained, manipulated, or indebted to you. Rather, devotion is focused, respectful attention given where it is welcomed, wanted, and can do the most good. It has little to do with rewards, although, in the end, the benefit is profound. Devotion and kindness go hand in hand—devotion adores, and kindness seeks the betterment of another person's experience or the relief of their discomfort.

PART TWO

Ordinary Kindness

If I had a friend and loved him because of the benefits which this brought me and because of getting my own way, then it would not be my friend that I loved but myself. I should love my friend on account of his own goodness and virtues and on account of all that he is in himself. Only if I love my friend in this way do I love him properly.*

—*Meister Eckhart*

* Meister Eckhart, *Selected Writings* (New York: Penguin Books, 1994), 119.

Kindness as Guidance

How Ordinary Kindness Guides Us to Make Important Life Choices

I was discussing with a friend how to be kind while at the same time remaining true to one's values. We talked about a story in the news from 2015 in which a Michigan motor mechanic apparently shared his intention not to work on cars of openly homosexual customers. Our discussion called into question the line where human or civil rights intersect with religious opinions: How can we make room for the diversity of ways of believing and still live according to our conscience and preserve each other's civil rights? We explored the role kindness played in navigating moral decisions, using same-gender marriage as a focus for our discussion.

Today, in our country, all people can become married legally and divorced legally. However, the religions of our nation have different ideas about whether or not that is okay. Fortunately, I do not have to believe in another person's religion. I'm free to have the opinion that marriage is a spiritual union and that divorce ought to be a spiritual separation, and that the state ought to have no say in the matter. My friend asked me if I would be willing to extend my professional services as a wedding officiant to all who come to me, to which I answered with a solid "yes." He probed deeper by asking whom I would feel personally challenged serving, whether it was performing a wedding or baking a cake. His questions gave me the opportunity to think about people who challenge me. Everyone has someone who challenges them. Even people who are deeply in love are tested from time to time by their partners. I would have been dishonest if I said that I always treat all people equally all the time. Sometimes when people challenge my patience, my commitment to kindness falters. When I am tired or overextended, it can take more energy than I seem to have to let kindness guide me. And when a situation arises that challenges my values, it can be tough to remember to be kind.

My friend continued with his questioning, asking me hypothetically if I would perform a wedding for a couple from out of town who turned out to be white supremacists and who had invited an all-white audience and wanted me to include words in the ceremony that reflected their belief. I became defensive quickly, arguing that being gay is not a choice, whereas being a white supremacist is optional. He asked me, "What would be the kindest thing to do?" We settled on the thought that being kind is not the same as being weak and that being kind is an attitude toward life that seeks the gentler path. However, the road of kindness will not necessarily be free from painful and difficult choices or significant discussions in which disagreement takes place. The hypothetical marriage got us thinking about our role models for kindness. We imagined what they would say in the situation. What would Buddha do? What would Jesus do? What would Mahatma Gandhi do? What would Dr. Martin Luther King, Jr. do?

There are clues in the stories of Jesus's life, such as the well-known story I mentioned earlier in this book about the prevailing

Mosaic law regarding adultery, which required an offender to be stoned to death. The story illustrates the challenge of making a choice based on law compared to making a choice based on compassionate kindness. In the story, the people who knew the laws tested Jesus. They wanted to see how he would respond to a clear-cut case of an adulterous woman and the legal punishment of stoning her to death. They likely knew the punishment was barbaric, and because they were aware that he had been an advocate for the kindly treatment of others, they were testing him. He resolved the matter by turning the situation back to them, saying, "Let you who is without sin be the first one to throw a stone." He would not condemn her. On one hand, his kindness to her in this incident is an example after which I would model my choices gladly. On the other hand, he was outspoken and unkind in a way that I have no desire to mimic. He became outraged on a visit to the temple where merchants had set up shop and turned the sacred place into a market. Some may think that his behavior was justified. However, as the Book of John reports, he fashioned a whip to drive them out and damaged their property, which is not a model for handling disagreement that I want to emulate. That response to disagreement is unkind. There has to be a better way. I do not think I ought to be permitted to treat people violently if they offend my values or my idea of Divinity. At the same time, I do not think religion or governments should require people to act against their conscience. Should authorities force Jehovah's Witnesses to receive blood transfusions in life-threatening situations? Should those who object be able to force women who choose to wear a burka to remove it? Should schools teach creation or evolution? Should barbaric laws about slavery or discipline from thousands of years ago apply to today? The line between human rights and religious thinking is wiggly right now, and the guidance one person receives from her faith tradition to answer these questions will not easily satisfy another person who has different values. The place where we meet is where we will find answers, and regardless of our religious convictions, what we have in common is that we are human. Humans love to love and be loved, and kindness crosses every boundary and will guide us into how to care about each other.

In the Bhagavad Gita, Krishna indicates that there are many paths to the ultimate goal of union with the Divine. The Quran suggests that different ways of believing *are* the will of the Divine. I take it all to mean that not everyone thinks the same way or travels the same path and that what works for me may not be right for another, and vice versa.

What Would Kindness Have Me Do?

I can imagine a world in which we are kind and compassionate to each other regardless of faith, nationality, gender, or political point of view. I can't see a way for that to come into being, though, if there are signs that hang on businesses announcing "No Episcopalians allowed," or "No heterosexuals allowed in this store," or "Christians not welcomed in this community," or "Divorced people not served in this restaurant."

A Catholic blog writer had some tough questions for her readers to consider when it comes to drawing moral lines. She made an excellent point about the challenge of maintaining consistency when refusing to do business with people based on differences in religious opinions. She asked her Catholic readers to consider what they would do if an unwed couple wants to celebrate their fifth anniversary of living together and they want a cake for their party. Should Catholic bakers bake the cake, or would the bakers' religious conscience forbid it? Would baking the cake be seen as giving tacit support to a lifestyle that they think negatively affects society? Similarly, would a Catholic florist arrange a flower bouquet for a "divorce party," or for a couple remarrying without an annulment? Or would it be more appropriate for the florist to decline the request based on the really clear Catholic teachings about divorce and remarriage? Moreover, if an unwed mother approaches a Catholic photographer for a portrait with her baby, what is the appropriate response? Does the Catholic photographer complete the portrait as an act of charity, or refuse on the basis of conscience?

The point she is making about consistency is compelling. I get it. If I am going to be judgmental, at least let me be consistent about it and not pick on the one group or individual who challenges me. Similarly, if I am going to be kind, can I try to be consistent about it and not pick the one group or individual that resonates with me? There are many paths on this life journey, and we humans are going to disagree on the details of how to live it. I can imagine a world in which people have the freedom to follow their way of believing without anyone's civil or human rights being affected. However, I can't imagine getting to that world without learning how to disagree kindly. What would Jesus do with people whose point of view was different from his? Putting aside his behavior in the temple market for a moment, we already have a good, solid example of what he recommended we do from the Sermon on the Mount, recounted in the Book of Matthew paraphrased here:

> *You have heard that it was said, "You shall love your neighbor and hate your enemy." But I say to you, love your enemies, bless those who curse you, do good to those who hate you, and*

> *pray for those who spitefully use you and persecute you, that you may be sons of your Father in heaven; for God makes the sun rise on the good and the bad, and sends rain on the just and on the unjust. For if you love those who love you, what's the benefit of that? Anyone can do the same.*

What would Buddha do? We already know by these words from chapter one of the Dhammapada:

> *All that we are is the result of what we have thought: it is founded on our thoughts; it is made up of our thoughts. If a man speaks or acts with an evil thought, pain follows him, as the wheel follows the foot of the ox that draws the carriage.*
>
> *All that we are is the result of what we have thought: it is founded on our thoughts; it is made up of our thoughts. If a man speaks or acts with a pure thought, happiness follows him, like a shadow that never leaves him.*
>
> *"He abused me, he beat me, he defeated me, he robbed me"—in those who harbor such thoughts hatred will never cease.*
>
> *"He abused me, he beat me, he defeated me, he robbed me"—in those who do not harbor such thoughts hatred will cease.*
>
> *For hatred does not cease by hatred at any time: hatred ceases by love; this is an old rule.*

My role models of kindness include people who are famous because of their extraordinary examples, as well as ordinary people who have used kindness as a way of living a meaningful life without seeking acclaim. Role models give us something to look up to as a possible way to live our lives. It can be a fortunate or unfortunate thing that the people we spend a lot of time with become our role models of a sort, because we inevitably and unwittingly mimic the behavior and values of the people around us. Their examples may be good or not, and because we are not able to choose our parents or siblings, or even the people we work with, it is important to be mindful about what behaviors we look up to and let shape us when we do have a choice.

Practice

WHAT WOULD YOU DO?

How would you respond if someone asked you to do something that challenged your conscience? Whose example would you be following when you made your choice? What would be the kindest thing to do? On the *Common Kindness* blog, the author invites us to take a moment to think about a leader we admire and asks these questions:

> *Is your leader involved in business or politics? Are they an entertainer or a role model? Do you know this person intimately, or only through the media? Did this person live in the past or are they alive now? Is this person a good role model for your family or friends? Would you like your children to grow up to be like this person? Do you aspire to become similar to this person? Is your leader kind?**

Try the questions on yourself: Am I a good role model for family or friends? Would I like children to grow up to be like me? Am I kind?

---

* *Common Kindness*, https://blog.commonkindness.com/2012/06/03/are-kind-leaders-role-models-or-overrated/.

Make a list of several people you admire, and try to identify the qualities about them that you admire. The resulting list will tell you something about what is important to you and how much of their role modeling is alive in you, influencing the way you treat other people.

Kindness Isn't Weakness

How Kindness Takes Courage

The kindest things to do may not be the easiest things to do. Take, for example, the responsibility of a music teacher who has an enthusiastic student who shows little progress or no talent. If the time comes to make an investment in further education or a more expensive instrument, is it kinder to withhold what the teacher knows, or is it kinder to tell the student that he is not cut out to be a musician? Communicating unpleasant information is part of life. It can be difficult because of the risks involved: I may get hurt or hurt someone, I may be embarrassed or embarrass someone, I may be rejected or cause someone to feel rejected. I have on occasion chosen the weaker path of avoidance and buried my head in the sand rather than do the stronger thing. Unfortunately, by avoiding the necessary conversations, I have caused more hurt rather than avoiding it. The more effective action is to trust kindness to show me the way through difficult communications. Being kind consistently takes courage and strength. Some think kindness is a sign of weakness and that a person must be blunt and forceful if they want to be strong. To me, real strength is the ability not to retaliate and not to attack when provoked. When I am at the mercy of my reactions, I am weak, because almost anything can set me off, and when I consistently allow myself to return unkindness for unkindness, I don't become stronger, I become more and more a slave to other people's unkindness. Nothing develops fear and resentment like treating people forcefully and rudely, and nothing promotes respect and closeness like treating others with genuine kindness. There is a difference between genuine kindness and pretend kindness. Pretend kindness has no authenticity behind it and is weak. For example, giving your kindness to people who are taking advantage of you, or bullying you, rather than establishing firm boundaries for yourself, is pretend kindness. Being kind does not mean agreeing with people who are behaving unkindly, and it doesn't mean going along quietly with unjust actions.

The English philosopher Thomas Hobbes thought that humans are naturally greedy, that we are driven by selfishness to get what we can, and that without governance, our nature would lead us to a state of war with each other. I don't agree. I don't think we need governance to force our hand to be kinder to each other. That is not to say there is no danger of succumbing to selfishness. I see that selfishness exists in me, and I see that it takes strength to turn away from it, and also to turn away from the inclination to gain an advantage over others. I prefer to think that kindness is one of the higher expressions that humans are naturally capable of. It requires strength to move away from childlike self-centeredness and toward kindness, because being kind makes us vulnerable to disappointment. That's why choosing kindness is not always easy, but it is possible. The actions of former members of radical right-wing organizations who have chosen a new life of kindness over hate inspire me. Life After Hate, a United States nonprofit organization, was created to support people who want to move on from a life of violence and racial discrimination.

*Life After Hate works to counter the seeds of hate we once planted. Through personal experiences and unique skill sets, we have developed a sophisticated understanding about what draws people to extremist groups and, equally important, why they leave. Compassion is the opposite of judgment, and we understand the roles compassion and empathy play in healing individuals and communities.**

Life After Hate's program EXITUSA supports people who are ready to leave the white power movement by providing information and support. Team members who were once part of the white power movement share their experience that it is possible to change and have a different life.

The consequence of making a change for kindness can have its challenges, as Linnaea Bohn, author of the blog *Tiny Buddha*, discovered. Linnaea ran into trouble in her corporate job because her kind and ethical treatment of the people she worked with did not match her supervisor's desired style of management. Even though the company's bottom line increased and Linnaea was given a promotion, her immediate supervisor saw her kindness as weakness and terminated her. This did not prevent her from following her natural inclination to be kind and helpful to others. She went on and volunteered to help Tibetan refugees develop small businesses to become economically self-sufficient. In her words, "Each kindness changes the world. Being kind is what makes my world significant."†

Ordinary kindness can be gritty, real, and authentic. It can help us grow stronger in our relationships, and it can guide us through tough communications. Kindness isn't about "making

---

* "Our History, Life After Hate," http://www.lifeafterhate.org/#!about/csgz.

† Linnaea Bohn, "Being Kind When It's Seen as a Weakness," *Tiny Buddha*, http://tinybuddha.com/blog/being-kind-when-its-seen-as-a-weakness/.

nice" to avoid upsetting people. It takes strength and commitment to find the kind way to be human. The advantage of doing so is that once we start being kind, the effects of it linger with us. It feels good. You might even experience the lightness of being that goes with spreading goodness. And as with anything that feels good, you will want to repeat the action that caused the good feeling. If you repeat it often enough, it may take over, and it may become your actual personality, and that may change your outlook on life.

Goodness as Kindness

How Kindness Is the Starting Point from Which Ordinary Goodness Flows

In the preface to *The Power of Kindness* by Piero Ferrucci, His Holiness the Dalai Lama wrote, "Kindness [is] the starting point, the fount from which flow so many other positive qualities, such as honesty, forgiveness, patience, and generosity." His words make me think about the connection between those positive qualities and kindness. What would honesty, forgiveness, patience, and generosity be without kindness? Is there even such a thing as unkind patience or unkind generosity or unkind honesty? In the case of so-called honest communication, I have experienced the truth wielded like an ax, but that is more of a heartless act of vendetta than it is an act of honesty. Telling the truth can be an act of kindness if the truth is told with sincerity and sensitivity.

Sincerity and sensitivity are keys to kindness. Sincerity includes being honest about my motives—in other words, being honest about my intentions before I speak, especially when addressing an unpleasant situation. When I have something difficult to communicate, I typically need to spend time searching my heart to discover if I have the other person's best interest in mind. I may find elusive mischief at play in the form of a subtle desire to put them down, to return a hurt or manipulate an outcome. I may even find a desire to get even or to get my way. Being sensitive to how sincere I am in my motives in communication helps me to be kinder. Sensitivity means that not only do I own my motive; I also take responsibility for the emotional aftermath of my interactions. Without this sensitivity, I might use the truth in a nasty way. I might disguise rudeness by calling it honesty. I might say such things as "I'm just speaking my truth" right before delivering a heartless opinion. Sensitivity means being considerate, and that is a kind way to be. It means being interested in finding the cleanest, gentlest way to say what I want to say, but with all mischief stripped away.

Even when you are sincere, there are no guarantees others will receive your communication in the manner in which you intended it. Nevertheless, these two qualities, sincerity and sensitivity, if I can be mindful enough to practice them, help me drop pretenses when engaging with others and help me to be kind. I love kindness, and like his Holiness the Dalai Lama, I too think of kindness as the best way to describe my religion. I am not a Christian in the common sense of the word, and I am not Jewish or Hindu or Muslim or pagan. However, anything in any of those religions that has to do with kindness inspires me and encourages me to learn more about that religion. If there is unkindness in a religion, I am less inclined to believe it is true or to trust that it can be helpful in living a good life. This is why the words of Jesus of Nazareth to his students have made an impression on me. He instructed them to love one another and advised them that the way they treat each other would be the telltale sign that they were his followers.

What do people know about me by observing the way I treat those around me? If, as I say it is, kindness is so important to me, and I love it and call it my religion, will people know that from observing me? Or will it be necessary for me to explain it? I made a decision a long time ago to act consciously as if kindness were important. I learned that not only *is* kindness important to me, it is also my greatest weakness. It seems that way because now if I commit an act of unkindness, I take it more seriously. If I am unkind, I feel disappointment more deeply than I do from most any other transgression. I am exploring kindness not only in my actions, but in my attitude also. I am trying to be more mindful of how I handle people and events in my thoughts. In some ways, it is the more challenging practice to be kind in thought than it is to be kind with actions and words. Nevertheless, it is a worthy project to let kindness guide me through the day. Especially if at times the idea of accessing goodness seems too difficult or unreachable, its gentler form of kindness can be a more accessible goal to reach for.

Shedding the Habit of Unkindness

In my parents' home, away from the warmth of my grandmother's kindness, I was immersed in a culture of sarcasm. Sarcasm was the standard mode of getting along with each other in my family. No one thought sarcasm was unkind. Rather, it was a sign of wit and engagement. It was how a person fit into the family. By the time I left my parents' home, sarcasm was imprinted on me and leaked out of every sentence I spoke. Out in the world, I discovered that sarcasm as a method of communication rarely accomplished what I thought it would. It did not break the ice, it did not defuse tension, it did not make a point well, it did not always win a debate, and in most cases, it did not unite me with others. Instead, sarcasm damaged my ability to connect with others, leaving an extensive emotional burn zone around me, on the other side of which were a growing number of people who doubted my sincerity and feared talking to me. The danger of sarcasm is that it alienates people and can hurt them. The turning point came when someone called me rude and condescending. Their accusation caused me to take an honest look at how I was presenting myself, and I came to the painful realization that I was indeed rude and condescending. I had always been. I began to see how sarcasm is unkind to both the one who uses it and those it is used on. I did not know how to stop it immediately. Rather, I struggled like a person trying to quit smoking—I wrestled daily, sentence by sentence, to strip mischief from my communication and suppress my sarcastic automatic reflexes.

I could not manage to quit sarcasm completely all at once. When I relapsed, I would tell myself that there is a time and place for everything, and that witty sarcasm can come out safely now and then—for example, when I am among close friends or with colleagues. It was how I coped with not succeeding at the amazingly difficult task of shedding the unkindness of sarcasm. Sometimes I was simply too lazy to find a more beautiful way to express myself and found it convenient to slip back into familiar modes of speaking. Nevertheless, I kept at it, and little by little, I was able to shed my reliance on sarcasm. I got to see how sarcasm could negatively affect people, and I got to see how they could thrive without it. The Greek word that is the origin of our word *sarcasm* means to tear flesh, and generally, definitions of the word point to the intent to hurt. Sarcasm brings tears to my eyes now and a dull, sick feeling when I witness other people using it, or when I sense it wanting to heave out of my mouth again after all these years of turning my back on it. I feel the same hurt and disappointment when I read message boards and comments sections on the Internet where sarcasm and blatant rudeness seem to be the typical ways people who don't know each other engage. I withdraw from adding my comments and remain quiet, not because I have nothing to say, but because I have not yet found a way to express myself that is consistent with kindness. Until I can say what I want to say kindly, I try not to say anything.

Kindness Gym

Technology has made it possible for us to connect in new ways and communicate at lightning speeds with people we have never met. With this sudden faux intimacy, some important communication skills are suffering in what turns out to be a fast and impersonal way of life. From behind a computer screen or gazing into a smart device, it is easy to dehumanize a person who might be reading our communication. When we dehumanize a person, we may see no reason to be thoughtful, kind, respectful, or gentle. Rather than flee entirely from participating in online communication, I have decided to let the world of e-communication become my kindness gym, where I get to work on getting stronger in my use of kindness and iron out the kinks in my communication style.

One of my sources of inspiration is a customer-service representative on a technology help forum who answers every rant against the company he works for as if he is responding to a beloved parent or dear friend. Apparently, there is nothing in life more frustrating, no greater indignation, than a device that does not work as expected or software that mysteriously malfunctions. Technology support forums are where angry users get to let out their frustrations with justified rage at the support staff, who may be responding from a continent away. The technological barrier can contribute to an environment in which both staff and customer become tense and snippy. Some representatives have apparently been trained to answer with stock phrases: "Thank you for contacting us. I'm sorry you're having difficulty. Do I understand that your question is [insert here the exact question the customer already asked]?" These kinds of answers lack something personal and can have the effect of further infuriating the already frustrated customer. My role model, when he replies to complaints, stays on the topic of the inquiry with direct and polite language. He bypasses any temptation to strike back or become defensive when customers hurl unkind words in his direction. I imagine that he must have raised children of his own, because tantrums don't distract him. Or maybe, I tell myself, he understands the pointlessness of focusing on other people's manners, grammar, attitude, or language when trying to solve problems. Or maybe he is in touch with his original goodness and understands that kindness is its reward.

One of the ideas in Zen Buddhism is that humans are essentially Buddhas, but they get distracted from their true nature. The idea suggests to me that when we take a closer look at ourselves, we can expect to find loving-kindness already there waiting to be invoked, and that it will remain with us as a possible expression wherever we go and no matter what we are doing. But we become distracted, and through neglect, our kindness muscle gets out of shape. What distracts us from our true nature? Being too busy in our thinking can, as can a too busy schedule. Or overly identifying with our physical appearance, possessions, or status can have this effect on us. Or indulging in unhealthy habits or staying in unwholesome situations, or yearning for unhealthy conditions. Or procrastination, or greed, envy, or jealousy, or anything similar that points out and away from self.

Being out of shape makes it difficult to return to normal, especially when the state of being out of shape feels more reasonable than the state of being fit. Imagine that for some reason you have let yourself get out of shape physically. When you decide, eventually, to get back into shape, you may not feel like doing so, even though aliveness and vitality feel good. Fitness may seem unnatural and require too much effort. Imagine that you have been slacking for some time now, eating poorly and being lazy for so long that it feels quite normal to you. Besides, everyone around you is in a similar state. It is the law of averages at work, and it seems to be winning.

Then one day you have an insight into your life, and you realize that you long to get back to your natural state. So you get started turning it around by taking a vigorous walk around the neighborhood, and it is wonderful. Except that it is also exhausting, and after the initial rush of endorphins released by your effort, your unprepared muscles suffer from the aches and pains that come from sudden vigorous exercise. Right then your mind may say, "I was better off watching TV and eating good food. At least *that* felt good." But imagine that you interrupt the train of thought and renew your decision to stick with getting fit, and you do get back into shape. It's wonderful, and you feel better and better about yourself because you can do things now that you forgot you were able to do. You realize that even the smallest investment in your physical well-being feels good and helps you experience your aliveness.

Getting started with workouts of any kind is the trick. We have to dive in to break the inertia. Opportunities to practice fill our lives, and there is no point in waiting for ideal circumstances or a revelation to nudge us into starting. Some people may delay beginning the practice of being kind because of the risk of being disappointed. After all, others may reject or misunderstand our kindness if they are not accustomed to receiving it from us. Others may struggle with the cultural idea that kindness is weakness and fear the possibility that people may take advantage of them and exploit their kindness. These vulnerabilities do exist, and simultaneously there are good reasons to persist and take the risk of diving into being kind.

Our loving-kindness can get out of shape too, from neglect,

even though we may think it to be our true nature. If we are out of shape long enough, it can appear to be more normal to be unkind than it is to be kind. Besides, it may be the case that few people around us are bothering to be kind. Movies, for example, often celebrate snarky, sarcastic, and vengeful heroes. It is easy to imagine that being that way is natural and reasonable. Imagine again that you have a moment of clarity, realizing that the real you is not like that and that your true nature is to be kind, and you decide one day to begin exercising your kindness muscles again. Like the first walk in the neighborhood to get fit, there may be an initial high from the first venture into kindness, but it's not all smooth sailing. This kindness workout takes more energy than you thought it would. Also, it does not feel natural right away. Your mind may say, "Oh, I was better off when I didn't have to pay attention to every word that came out of my mouth. It was easier reserving harsh words for a few select people." But you interrupt that train of thought, and you stick with kindness and practice it daily. Then eventually you get to a level of competence where you realize it does not take energy to be kind at all. Rather, being kind releases energy, all types of energy. It is like coming home to your natural, authentic self, and you discover an endless resource of vitality.

I can get out of shape in the way I think about appropriate communication and how much I want kindness to govern my actions. When I do, I remember the customer service representative, my role model of kindness. When I want to comment on a controversial topic on a message board or online newspaper article, I think of his example. It is disheartening to realize that without sarcasm or a jab at someone's logic, I frequently have nothing left to say. It is heartening, however, to notice that I have become less inclined to be unkind. In the growing complexity of our world, information overload is increasing, making it difficult to stay rooted in kindness. As beautiful as technology is, it can cause people to feel isolated. Social media gives the illusion of connecting, but it cannot replace what happens between people when they sit together and talk. I read a comic strip in which three people show up for a funeral. One of the attendees commented, "I expected a better turnout; she had 3,000 friends on Facebook." The act of being physically together and talking for no other reason than to connect is being lost. I was talking to a young man on the phone about an emotional breakup he was going through. As the conversation progressed, he became agitated with remembered sadness, and at one point, he said: "Edward, can't we just text; this is too painful to talk about."

Without the warmth of being present physically with each other, it is easier for our connections to be heartless. I was reading an online newspaper about a tragic shooting that took place in our country—and the comments section was particularly eye-opening. As I read the comments, I wondered if the authors of the sharp-tongued words would say such things to each other in person. Somehow, because a computer screen separated those commenting from the event, they appeared to feel no connection to the victims in the story. Their words were careless and unkind. Email can have a similar effect of dehumanizing the people on either end of the communication. I have practiced using email in the same way that I learned to write a letter. I try to insert a proper salutation at the beginning of emails and to begin the conversation with some sincere and connecting question. I do this both to slow down my racing mind and to avoid the casualties that can come from careless lapses of kindness. I do it also to convey respect and caring. I realize this practice is not always practical or appropriate when you have something urgent to attend to and need to get to the point directly. However, those circumstances are far less frequent than I allow myself to believe, and typically there is a way to bring kindness into my communication.

I do not like heartless communication, even when it is a time-sensitive business matter. The more I know about the person I am communicating with, the harder it is for me to withhold kindness. The less I know about the person's personal life, their dreams and challenges, the easier it is for me to dehumanize them. That is why a conversation in real time—in person—is so important. Intimacy requires being present and promotes closeness, and with closeness comes kindness. We like being with people who are kind to us, and people like being with us when we are kind. It is easier to overlook differences with people who are kind when we collaborate.

Kindness as Attitude

How Kindness Is One of the Many Options Available All the Time

I had not thought of kindness as a religion until I read the Dalai Lama's statement that his simple religion is kindness. Thinking of kindness as a religion elevated it to something more important than an optional attribute. I understand religion to mean "that which binds" or obligates us, something taken so seriously that it becomes an attitude or a way of thinking that is reflected in a person's character. Kindness became increasingly important to me, and the more I expressed it, the more I enjoyed it, and the more I enjoyed it, the more I wanted to share it so others could benefit from it. Cultivating an attitude of kindness is stress-reducing and helps me feel in harmony with my world. However, it is also quite easy to abandon. I learned how easy it is for small errors of judgment that everyone makes to cause us to abandon kindness. These little jealousies and deceits that we muddle through and work out are part of the landscape of life. They are not of great concern when we correct them. Only when they are allowed to take root and displace kindness do they become worrisome. When I am kind, I am less worried and move through the world with confidence and peace. When I am kind, I'm more inclined to act honestly, with forgiveness, patience, generosity, respect, and consideration. When I am not kind, I am inclined to be inconsiderate, disrespectful, or insensitive. And whatever attitude I indulge the most—kind or unkind—becomes increasingly more reasonable and normal to me.

"Entrainment" is a term that refers to the process by which interacting oscillating systems assume the same rhythm, like the "odd kind of sympathy" Christian Huygens described between pendulum clocks he was studying: when mounted close to each other on the same support board, clocks would often become synchronized.* We have a similar tendency that can be observed in a bar or at a party where loud, rhythmic music is playing. We sometimes begin to tap our fingers or feet or nod our heads unconsciously to the rhythm of the music, giving the room a strange kind of synchronized aliveness. Or when we regularly keep company with a group of people, sometimes we take on each other's speech patterns. The upside of this tendency to entrain with each other is that it suggests we can pick up the beneficial habits of those we hang out with. The downside is that when we are unaware of the rhythm or tone of a group, or of the environment we spend a lot of time in, we can pick that up too.

When we become aware of the freedom we have to choose what we synchronize with, that awareness is liberating. The clock pendulums may not be able to ask "What will I resonate with today?," but you and I can. I have found it beneficial to think about what I am letting myself become synchronized to. It's both rewarding and exciting to pay attention to how life changes when we take note of and synchronize with kindness. I have been

---

* Christian Huygens, letter to the Royal Society, in *Oeuvres Completes de Christian Huygens*, vol. 5, edited by M. Nijhoff (The Hague: Société Hollandaise des Sciences, 1893), 246.

dabbling with learning to play the harp over the past several years, and for many months at a time, my harp stands neglected in the corner of my office. I've noticed that it is highly sympathetic to the noises around it and will vibrate with other sounds. Even if a bus passes by, the beautifully sensitive soundboard will resonate with the vibrations of the passing vehicle. It has no choice in doing so. Even though I believe I have a choice, sometimes I behave like the soundboard on a harp. I hear a piece of news I don't particularly like, and I let it send its vibration through me. Someone in my circle of friends behaves a certain way, and I let myself match their attitude before I think about it and how I want to respond. Reducing these automatic responses has been significant for me in cultivating an attitude of kindness. Although I am not skilled in purposefully choosing what I will feel at a moment's notice, I am becoming better at interrupting the tendency to go with the crowd, because I have learned to pause and to think about what is stimulating my emotions. That second of suspension can be exactly what is needed for me to recalibrate to kindness. When consciously practiced, an attitude of kindness attunes the one practicing it to the expression of kindness around them. They may find themselves becoming aware of much more goodness than they realized is in our world, and that, in turn, may stimulate them into even greater expressions of kindness too. Practicing kindness makes us happy, and allowing unkindness to go uncorrected makes us unhappy. Whether we practice daily acts of kindness, or unkindness, whatever we choose will become a welcome guest in us and will eventually take up permanent residence.

Kindness as a Habit

What Daily Kindness Looks Like

The United Kingdom dedicates one day annually, November 13, to celebrate and promote kindness. Observers of Kindness Day coordinate events such as distributing thousands of candy bars at train stations, encouraging a nationwide wave of kindly feelings, and recognizing children for deeds of kindness with public awards. November 13 is also World Kindness Day, promoted by the World Kindness Movement.* It is observed in many countries with projects such as huge public hugging events, and distribution of gifts, as well as ceremonies recognizing kindness. Once a year is not bad to start with, but developing kindness into a daily habit requires paying attention to it and introducing more acts of kindness regularly into your days. To start, here are some suggestions from the World Kindness Movement's resource page: bring a treat to the office for your coworkers, write a note to a colleague or teacher with words of appreciation, be polite online, say something nice to someone, pick up garbage on a hiking trail,

* World Kindness Movement, http://www.theworldkindnessmovement.org/.

compliment the waitstaff at a restaurant, bring in the neighbor's empty trash container, volunteer at a food bank, become an organ donor, adopt a highway, leave quarters at a laundromat, donate your hair.

Introducing focused exercises such as these on a daily basis can bring kindness into a person's life in a powerful way and help establish it as a beneficial habit. But what stops a person from being kind on a regular basis? For some, it may be the risk of being disappointed by misunderstanding or rejection. For others, kindness, as we've heard before, is equated with weakness. The prospect of being taken advantage of may block their willingness to be kind. Here are some cautions about practicing kindness that can help as you navigate around some of these concerns:

1. **Don't express kindness to get it.** An attitude of "giving to get" sabotages the kindness. Rather, show kindness because it is ordinary to you—natural. Don't express kindness to gain anything from it. Express it because it's a good thing to do.
2. **Don't withhold kindness until you are confident it will be reciprocated.** You might wait forever. Think of the kindness you withhold from others as kindness you withhold from yourself. Kindness will make you happier when you indulge in it. You'll feel good when you do good things. David R. Hamilton, PhD, author of *I Heart Me: The Science of Self-Love*, says that on a biochemical level, it is believed that the good feelings that come from being kind are due to elevated levels of the brain's natural version of morphine and heroin—in other words, kindness causes a natural high.*

---

* David R. Hamilton, "5 Beneficial Side Effects of Kindness," Huffington Post, June 2, 2011, http://www.huffingtonpost.com/david-r-hamilton-phd/kindness-benefits_b_869537.html.

3. **Don't compare how you express kindness with how other people express it.** Rather, trust your ordinary kindness to inspire you to achieve warm and genuine ways of expressing it. Pay attention to the feeling you get when you are kind. Typically, it is a warm feeling of emotional well-being.

Expressing gratitude regularly is an easy and effective way to bring kindness into play on a daily basis. The nonprofit organization I work for makes a point of sending thank-you cards to people who make a contribution of any amount. One recipient contacted the staff to let us know she did not need the thank-you cards, saying, "That's not why I give." The purpose of the card writing, however, reaches beyond that person's need, into the heart of our organizational values, in that we aim to be mindful of never falling into heartless receiving, taking people's generosity for granted and forgetting the importance of kindhearted gratitude. We write thank-you cards because we want to be sure that we do not dehumanize our givers. So we have made a commitment to write thank-you cards wherever we see an opportunity for one. A donor reported to me that when she received an envelope from our organization with a card in it, she opened it, thinking to herself, "Okay, what do they want now?" But she found no self-addressed, stamped return envelope and no solicitation of funds, only a genuine expression of gratitude. She said, "It touched me deeply. I've been back to the card several times to look at it." Later she told me that receiving the card inspired her to write to her family members who lived in other states, communicating to them what she appreciated about them.

Kindness is contagious. When we get into it, the warmth and excitement are infectious to others around us.

Notwithstanding the vulnerabilities that go with being kind, there are also good reasons to pursue it. Neurophysiologist James

W. Prescott, in a study of forty-nine cultures, concludes among other things that high levels of physical affection shown to children are associated with lower levels of violence. Affection apparently reduces the incidence of crime, murder, killing, and the torturing of enemies.* Treating infants kindly, it seems, may be one of the best and easiest ways to transform our culture of isolation and violence into one of peace. Even if there are no infants in your life, you can apply daily doses of kindness to adults, animals, and possibly even objects—all of which respond very well when treated kindly. Those who express kindness benefit as much as those who receive it. Nevertheless, to show kindness for the purpose of personal benefit steals something from the process. Kindness is a commitment to generosity, not to personal gain.

Kindness conveys caring. Humans, animals, and plants flourish with regular expressions of care. It is possible to survive without it, but a caring touch, a sincere handshake, or a friendly hug does wonders because of the warmth communicated by such ordinary acts of kindness. Practicing kindness daily does not need to be any more complicated than a genuine smile, an act of service, spending quality time with someone, or engaging in a conversation and listening generously. The first tip above advises us not to give kindness simply in order to receive it in return. However, you can be sure you will receive something good in return: the warm, full feeling of having contributed something to our world.

We ought not to feel emptied by expressing kindness. If you do feel drained, you may not be showing true kindness. Kindness ought to be natural, easy, and satisfying. Also, we ought not to feel icky as a result of receiving what someone thinks is kindness—for example, the expressions of an invasive hugger or a person who talks at you without consideration for your time. Sometimes I

---

* James W. Prescott, "Body Pleasure and the Origins of Violence," *The Futurist*, April 1975.

want to shut down and withdraw from people as a result of a few of those awkward experiences, fearing that they characterize all interactions with that person. In reality, it is not that we are drowning in kindness in this world, but rather there seems to be an enormous opportunity to express more of it on a daily basis. Still, sometimes silence and solitude are necessary to refuel the tanks from which your kindness draws its power. It is a kind and healthy thing to know when you need to take time for yourself to replenish.

Practice
Say Something Genuinely Kind

Try this simple exercise: Give someone in your life a sincere compliment by recognizing what they do well. It might be one of their routine tasks, such as completing homework or locking up the office mindfully at the end of the workday. Or it could be a good habit that is easy to overlook because of its consistency. For example, if a partner regularly cleans up after you enjoy a meal together, practice mentioning that you notice and appreciate it.

The caveat for this experiment to be successful is that it has to be completely genuine and unaffected. Think of it as a "drive-by complimenting"—something mentioned in passing. Although you may put some thought into it, the delivery ought to be as natural as brushing your teeth or drinking a glass of water so as to keep it simple and unaffected. But do make sure the compliment is a sincere appreciation. Otherwise, the experiment will fail.

Relationship coach Dr. Ellen Kreidman suggests that this technique can be used to validate appreciated behavior in partners or children. Rather than focusing on and correcting frustrating behavior, redirect your attention to appreciation. It is a commitment to patience, because you may find, as many people discover, that abandoning the strong urge to correct or criticize is not that easy to achieve. Regularly focusing on what the people in my life do well develops generosity of spirit in both them and me: I become more inclined to notice their good habits and qualities, and they, in turn, feel joyful and willing to repeat the activity that was appreciated.

Turn the spotlight on ordinary acts of kindness by talking about them when you notice them. Social media is an excellent vehicle for the practice. Make a goal of updating your daily status for a week on your favorite social media site or on your blog, if you have one, mentioning an act of kindness you witnessed each day.

Make a Pledge

The Be Kind People Project™ teaches children what it means to be kind by enrolling them in a personal pledge in the form of a small card that they can carry around with them to help keep them on the kindness track.* The project provides those who enroll with easy-to-follow guides and examples of how kindness can be expressed easily, such as: be encouraging, be supportive, be positive, be helpful, be honest, be considerate. Kindness, the project teaches, is a force without force and quite possibly the way to create beneficial social change in school and in society. You can create your kindness pledge by making a list of actions that represent what being kind means to you. Print it on a small card and share it. Consider or elaborate on such phrases as "I pledge to be reassuring, courteous, grateful, supporting," etc.

When you practice kindness, keep in mind that dealing with strangers takes wisdom and maturity. Not everyone will receive

---

* "Take the Be Kind Pledge," Kind: The Be Kind People Project, http://www.thebekindpeopleproject.org/take-kind-pledge-page.html.

your kindness kindly, and some may be tempted to get more from you than you first intended to give. Nevertheless, the risk of these outcomes ought not to discourage you from trying. A good tip is not to take your acts of kindness too seriously. Try to have as few expectations as possible—get into the act for the act itself.

My Thoughts Are with You

Kindness can be practiced privately and silently. For example, practice thinking kindly about people in your life. You might discover at first a tendency to trip over what you think are their weaknesses, and if you bring yourself gently back to thinking kindly about people, it will do something to your attitude toward them—and possibly they will feel the change in you. Try practicing this way at the end of each day. You might do it directly before going to sleep. Start, for example, with bringing into your awareness the last person you encountered in your day. Identify something you appreciate about them. Then move on to the person you encountered before that and bring into your awareness something you appreciated about them. Not only is this a joyful practice, but it also promotes peacefulness and sound sleep. If you struggle to find something about a person to appreciate because of some tension between the two of you, try focusing on a habit of theirs. You might find you can appreciate their neatness or the way they handle their colleagues. It is helpful, for this practice, to remember Samuel Johnson's idea that the true measure of a person is how they treat someone who can do them no good.

Kindness as Listening Generously

How Deep Listening Leads to Compassion

I saw a cartoon strip once in which a little girl looks up at her father, who is reading the newspaper, and says, "Dad, you have to listen to me with your eyes as well as your ears." Listening generously means listening wholeheartedly, with your mind and an attitude of openness. Simply hearing and processing words is not always enough. Indeed, I learned from my grandmother that, even when she didn't understand the words I was saying when I described some modern invention or current problem, she listened to me and followed me without always understanding the details. Listening is a physical process, and it is also an interpretive, sensed experience that synthesizes the nonverbal elements of communication, such as tone of voice, facial expressions, gestures, and other cues. When she listened to me, she would look at me—head tilted forward and eyes wide open.

Listening, or "real" hearing, must include a relationship—an interaction between the receiver and the transmitter. A good listener is a good receiver. I haven't always been a good receiver. Most of my young adult life, I was more of a broadcaster than a receiver. I talked *at* people in conversation, and my thoughts dwelt on my needs and desires rather than on what the person was saying. When I became willing to *hear*, I discovered a whole new world of information about people and myself. My world and my relationship to life became expanded. When I couldn't hear, I missed so many of the details and subtleties of what was happening around me because I didn't yet know how to listen mindfully. In a conversation, I seemed to be more interested in filling up the silences with questions, opinions, and answers than I was in learning anything. In that style of listening, there wasn't enough silence to hear, not sufficient space, and there was too much rushing ahead to contribute the next idea. Many people don't actually listen—instead, they are waiting for their turn to speak, mentally planning their response. When that is the case, it's difficult to hear well.

In one of those day-by-day desk calendars with daily inspirational quotes, I came upon a page that I stayed with for a week because the message was so touching: "It's hard to tune in to Heaven's message if our lives are full of earthly static." It was a helpful reminder at the time to be mindful of the static in my head caused by being overly concerned with preparing answers while other people were still speaking. I would often interrupt their speaking so that I could hurry on to what I had to say, telling myself I had heard enough of what was being said, that I thoroughly understood and needed to get to what was crucial: my wisdom. Looking back at how I engaged with the world around me during those times, it seems it was like trying to understand a complex novel by reading only a sentence here or there. This practice of not hearing and not listening developed into a tendency to reject quickly, generalize, and jump to a conclusion.

When I listened through my bias that I knew all the answers about a topic, I closed myself off to new ideas and let my confidence in my current level of study get in the way of actually listening. I would find myself quickly dismissing people. I was also not able to pick up cues from life that could assist me in flourishing. I like to think of life as filled with new information and helpful promptings. But it might as well not be if I don't pay attention and don't allow myself to listen to it, and if I don't allow other people to be heard.

Brother Lawrence, a seventeenth-century monk, advised us to do everything in life as if it were an act of worship.* This advice has been helpful in deepening the way I listen to people and to life. I imagine that what I'm listening for is crucial indeed. When I am having difficulty remaining present, I use my imagination to improve my listening by asking myself, "How would I conduct my listening if this were a person like Buddha or Jesus or Dr. Martin Luther King, Jr. before me?" I tell myself that I would probably look at them in a focused way. I would probably pay attention. I would probably listen. It's possible I would even be willing to be enriched by what I was hearing. When I practice mindfully listening in this way, it reminds me of how my grandmother listened. I don't know what her internal process was, but I do know that her attention to my speaking left an indelible mark on my memory and has served as an encouragement to work toward being mindfully present for others.

Practice
Tell Me More

Pick someone to practice listening to. Begin your conversation with a question that is easy for them to answer and doesn't require too much personal information. An example of a simple conversation

---

* Brother Lawrence, *The Practice of the Presence of God* (New Kensington, PA: Whitaker House, 1982). "We ought not to be weary of doing little things for the love of God, who regards not the greatness of the work, but the love with which it is performed."

starter question is, *Have you seen any good movies lately?* The question requires only a yes or no answer. If the person you are practicing on wants to offer more information, they most likely will. You can follow up by asking a question that is likely to receive a more complete response. For example, *What did you think of it?* Think of questions that seek the person's opinions or feelings. Another example is *How did that make you feel?* Or *What is your opinion about the quality of the movie?*

Asking these open-ended questions gives you the opportunity to listen to people, their ideas and feelings. If you ask questions that require only a one-word answer, you may find yourself driving the content of the conversation. *Would you recommend the movie? Did you like the movie? Was it a good movie?* Each of these questions has the possibility of bringing the conversation to an end with a yes/no response. Instead, try to use questions that ask what people think, feel, and believe and then listen to their responses without interrupting them.

PART THREE
Ordinary Compassion

No one knows better what heat is than someone who is hot. No one knows better what wisdom is than someone who is wise, and no one knows better what eternal life is than eternal life itself.*

—*Meister Eckhart*

---

* Meister Eckhart, *Selected Writings* (New York: Penguin Books, 1994), 209.

The Compassion of Wanting to Understand

Beyond Borders: Empathy

"Travel," Mark Twain wrote, "is fatal to prejudice, bigotry, and narrow-mindedness, and many of our people need it sorely on these accounts. Broad, wholesome, charitable views of men and things cannot be acquired by vegetating in one little corner of the earth all one's lifetime."* Nowadays, we can travel to places around the world without leaving our one little corner. We can explore distant cultures on the Internet, with Google Maps and Wikipedia. But if you have a desire to grow in understanding of what others are dealing with, it takes a willingness to travel beyond online experiences. To explore what inner borders we may have, and to discover where we may have become narrow-minded, we have to take in and consider points of view that are different from our own. The goal has to be to understand the other point of view instead of to debate it or correct it. Compassion depends on this.

---

* Mark Twain, *The Innocents Abroad* (New York: Penguin Books, 2002).

I spent some time trying to understand the Israel-Palestine conflict by educating myself with online resources. It wasn't until I spoke to people on opposing sides of the conflict that I began to feel the painful wounding of experiences that seemed impossible to understand. I wanted to get beyond the routine American news services and broaden my understanding. I researched the history of the two countries. I read user comments on articles representing different points of view. I read blogs, travel guides, and online news articles. My hope was to come to a definitive opinion and understanding of the situation. I was trying to find a side to take and land on it squarely. What I found instead was a complex and painful problem. The more informed I became, the less clear I was. I learned that I had a tendency to avoid reading uncomfortable points of view that upset me. But without them, I limited myself to familiar, comfortable territory. I learned that to avoid the discomfort of understanding someone's pain, I tended to oversimplify subjects and avoided learning about them. When surfing the wave of popular media, it was very easy to let myself be told what to think, what is important to learn about, and what is not. Take, for example, the terrorist attacks in France in November 2015. At approximately the same time, terrorism in Beirut left many dead and wounded, and earlier in the year more than one hundred children were shot in Kenya. However, social media in November focused on France. Facebook offered users the option to change their profile picture so that it featured a watermarked French flag as a sign of solidarity. Unless I missed it, no such sympathy was shown to the victims of the Kenyan university shooting or the bomb blasts in Beirut. I wondered what it might be like for a family member of a Kenyan victim to witness the massive outpouring of love and support to Paris from across the world while the Kenyan tragedy went relatively unnoticed.

Roman Krznaric, a faculty member of the School of Life in London, is an expert on empathy. He describes it as a habit that can be cultivated to improve the quality of our lives and the lives of people around us. We can develop empathy by adopting new practices, such as developing curiosity about strangers, challenging prejudices, and discovering commonalities among people—seeing life through someone else's eyes and listening deeply. He defines empathy as "the ability to step into the shoes of another person, aiming to understand their feelings and perspectives, and to use that understanding to guide our actions. That makes it different from kindness or pity."* Empathy, then, is the effort to find what is relevant and meaningful to others, what makes them tick, as well as what makes them purr, growl, hurt, and sing. We may not agree or have similar feelings, but we get it. It is an expression of ordinary goodness, and it allows us to reach beyond the borders that separate people so that we can understand and care about each other. When we let ourselves stay open to understanding what other people are experiencing, our empathy will be invoked through our shared experience, and we begin to connect and care about each other. We have to be open to the full experience, though, not only the parts we already resonate with. We can't be fully empathetic if we shy away from what is unpleasant. Compassion is empathy plus the desire to make a helpful contribution.

The original meaning of compassion was limited to suffering with another. Toward the end of the fourteenth century, the meaning expanded to include emotions such as anger and love. I keep that in mind when I am trying to understand another person's experience. I attempt to remember that empathy means being willing

---

* Roman Krznaric, "Six Habits of Highly Empathic People," *Kindness Blog*, January 20, 2015, https://kindnessblog.com/2015/01/20/six-habits-of-highly-empathic-people-by-roman-krznaric/.

to take in their joy and disappointment, their hopes and dreams, and also the confused expression of everything all at once, because I want to make a difference. That can be difficult in this positive-thinking culture. It can be frightening to acknowledge the reality of another person's pain, or suffering, or anger, or confusion. Perhaps we are afraid of facing our own pain, and pity sets in, creating a barrier between us. Pity accepts the futility of a situation, whereas empathy embraces the situation without seeking immediate resolution. Pity places the other person in a lesser status, whereas empathy brings us closer together with respect and understanding. It can be scary for me to be empathetic when I don't think that I have enough personal resources to handle the experience emotionally. When I fear I am going to be overwhelmed by the other person's feelings, I try to remember that it is natural to resonate with another person's emotion, and natural to feel disturbed by someone else's suffering or elated by their joy. That is the risk we take when loving each other. Thomas à Kempis reminds us that "Love feels no burden, thinks nothing of trouble, attempts what is above its strength, pleads no excuse of impossibility; for it thinks all things lawful for itself and all things possible."*

On a visit to San Diego, a friend invited me to see the local zoo, one of the finest in the world. I felt acutely uncomfortable about viewing caged wild animals. I had not enjoyed visiting zoos in the past and remembered feeling miserable seeing animals kept in enclosures that can never mimic their natural habitat. My friend explained that the zoo raised many animals for reintroduction into the wild. Even so, I did not want to go. I felt the same feeling I get when I am about to visit someone in the hospital who is suffering—I feel afraid to let in the whole situation. I'm afraid that I will not

---

* Thomas à Kempis, *Imitation of Christ*, vol. 49 (London: Oxford University Press, 1903).

be able to do anything about what I am witnessing and that the situation will overpower me.

My friend pressed on, explaining that the zoo, using science-based methods, was leading the way in conservation of endangered animals and had impressive success. He mentioned that I might be limiting my experience by being unwilling to consider new information. I took a deep breath and accepted his invitation to the zoo. It turned out to be a profoundly interesting and inspiring visit. It also stirred up unpleasant feelings. That is what we might get when we let ourselves feel and understand the world around us: gritty, complex, and not easily resolvable feelings. At the zoo I saw an exotic wild cat, sitting there majestically, with hordes of people chatting, grinning, snapping photos seemingly without appreciation. Then the crowd moved on to the next display with what to me was insufficient awe at what they had seen. It occurred to me that life can be like that: the miraculous reduced to entertainment, sterilized so that war is a news story on television and talk shows, and aging is something that happens in a convalescence home. But because I risked feeling my discomfort, I was able to take in the whole experience and understand the tragic trade-off: captivity for conservation. I value saving species worldwide through conservation science, while I also struggle with unnatural environments for wild animals. The visit made me open up the barrier my past experiences had formed around my thinking. It didn't, however, make it any easier to take in.

How to Be Empathetically Present for Another Person

A significant challenge in our society is that many people live solitary lives. They may have fragile connections to community through the Internet, texting, and social media. Verbal skills seem to be on the decline. Short, quick messages are increasingly becoming the way to communicate. Many people sit staring at computer screens typing for longer and longer periods. I cannot stress enough the importance of a regular, scheduled time to interact with other people, both in family circles and beyond. It is increasingly important to make the effort to create meaningful connections with other people in real-time situations where we can interact face-to-face. I picked up some excellent, compassionate listening skills from a training program where I learned to give emotional support to people diagnosed with terminal diseases. In the training, volunteers learned how to listen actively to both the words the client spoke and the meaning behind the words. We learned how to listen without formulating an opinion, evaluating, or giving advice. Our goal for listening was to try to understand the other person's frame of reference. We practiced listening for the expression of feelings by paying attention to repeated ideas and emphasized words. One training exercise had us tell emotionally charged stories to each other. Two by two, we sat in chairs with our backs facing each other. One trainee told a story while the other tried to listen attentively, which proved to be difficult while facing the opposite direction. After the exercise, we discussed our experience. Participants reported a feeling of being disconnected from the person who was speaking because they could not see them. We felt frustrated by the challenge of paying attention to what our partner was saying because we could not take in the speaker's facial expressions and other nonverbal cues without visual contact. The speakers, too, reported a reduction in the feeling of being well understood. Some trainees noticed a strong urge to break away from the back-to-back formation and wanted to reach around to the other person to make eye contact and show that they were present, interested, and caring.

The point of the exercise was to help us identify how to be

empathetically present for another person. We brainstormed helpful ideas to keep in mind when listening to another person:

- Begin with ordinary caring. Imagine that what you are about to receive by listening is similar to receiving a valuable gift.
- Think about the courage and/or vulnerability that may be necessary for the one speaking to divulge what they are about to say.
- Listen with kindhearted interest. In other words, try to notice when you begin categorizing what you hear as good or bad, right or wrong, and try to return to ordinary listening.
- Be sensitive to the communication that comes through the whole experience and not only to the words being spoken. Listen for the expression of feelings.

When I listen in this way, the result is powerful, both for the person I am listening to and for me. I create a meaningful connection with people I listen to in this way, and they report having the feeling of being understood. I jokingly tell others that the less I say, the wiser I appear to be. But it isn't entirely a joke—the less I say, the more space there is for other people to express themselves. Having the freedom to express themselves to another person helps them sort through complex situations. Because I listen without interrupting, they feel unhurried.

When the socially challenged scientist Sheldon Cooper, on *The Big Bang Theory*, encounters distressing emotions, he typically says something like "Social convention dictates that I offer you a refreshing beverage." I think of my grandmother's gesture of tea in similar situations. Both gestures remind me that we don't have to be skilled or comfortable to be present for another person. Indeed, we may feel like fleeing when things become tender, sad, or emotional. Witnessing someone's distress may be awkward and cause us to feel inept or uncomfortable responding. That may be a correct observation—we may not have much experience. However, we have something: ordinary compassion. When we stay in the conversation despite our discomfort, the act of staying is what connects us to other people's experience and makes us empathetic. It may cause us to leave our comfort zone, but staying with a person conveys confidence and trust.

The emotional support service for people facing terminal diseases that I volunteered for paired me with a vibrant, opinionated, boisterous man whose diagnosis threw his life into chaos. I am introverted and quiet when meeting people for the first time, and he was not. At our first meeting, he pulled out all the stops and started sharing sensitive information, asking questions, making plans, and discussing problems all at once in a jumble of disconnected sentences. I sat quietly taking it in, not so much because I had learned that skill, but because it was my first assignment and I was terrified. I sat still and quiet because there was no opening to speak, and I didn't know what to say in response to the largeness of what he was dealing with. Later he reported to my supervisors that my skilled listening made him feel supported because I clearly had confidence in his ability to work through the messy emotions at a time when he lacked confidence in himself. His review of my service was astounding to me because after meeting with him I was plagued by the thought that I had failed to say anything useful at all. It turns out that my steadfast eye contact, although inspired by insecurity and inexperience, was communicating something to the client, and there wasn't anything more meaningful I could have contributed. He said he felt supported by the presence of someone who listened steadily. He later shared with me that typically people found him overwhelming and intense and that my ability to stay with him through his volcanic-eruption-like emotional expressions helped him immensely.

Good, compassionate listening, it turns out, is patient listening. People in distress may take a while to find appropriate words to describe their experience. Their emotions may be moving faster than they can find words to attach to them. Patience can help us to wait for them to sort it out without interjecting suggestions or cutting them off. Good listening is attentive listening in which the one listening abandons their smartphone and does not glance down to read a text message. A good listener renounces the world for the moment and focuses wholly on the person with them.

I have found great value in becoming aware of my listening style. I have discovered that there is a relationship between the way I listen to people and the way I listen to life and its intuitive prompts. When my mind is too busy with speaking and asserting points of view, I am not available to receive the wealth of information that life is full of. Like the notes of good music, our thoughts ought to have lots of spaces between them, places to breathe, to receive, and to listen. To receive the message that life is broadcasting, it may be necessary to reduce sensory input—for example, by limiting television viewing for a while, going without a smartphone for a day, leaving the books for a moment, and stepping into the solitude of doing nothing but listening. Without this kind of nourishing solitude, my ability to be present for others is severely reduced. My capacity to be compassionately present for others deteriorates when I don't take time for stillness. When I step away from the stimulations of life and close my eyes for a moment, I discover that my mental noise reduces also, and the conversations in my mind slow down. It gives me a chance to catch my breath and turn my attention kindly to the world within with the same compassion and attentiveness that I have used when listening to people.

Practice

Do Talk to Strangers

Try this. Develop the habit of talking to strangers as Roman Krznaric suggests, with a mind to deeply listen to them. This is an adult skill that can be a fun exercise if approached with flexibility and maturity. I have been experimenting during my regular walk around a local lake by greeting everyone who walks the same path in the opposite direction to me. It's entertaining to watch the variety of responses—from delight to suspicion. But developing curiosity about people you don't know has to be more than a greeting on a path. It has to be more than small talk, although that can be a good place to start, and it has to be kind. Nothing fails like launching twenty questions on someone you've never met before without any warm-up to the conversation. This kindness technique is practiced by being interested in people, and it's best conducted with class. Be classy about it. Don't be obnoxious. Don't do it with intense stalker energy, but rather approach it with a desire to learn more and to understand more. Don't worry about correcting any wrong information the other person might share, and don't be overly interested in sharing your point of view—instead, put your opinions on hold for a bit.

Sometimes when I get nervous or shy, I begin to talk aimlessly, and it effectively becomes me talking *at* people. The goal of this exercise to me would be to expand my awareness of other people's lives; not only that, it's useful in relieving the rampant loneliness that is part of being in the world today.

Here is how I envision the assignment. Talk to someone new every day, or to someone you don't know very well. Don't talk *at* them. Be gentle and kindly curious about them. Be brave and willing to accept a lukewarm response—and, if you do, move on. When the person you choose does respond, practice listening to them openheartedly. Try as best you can to be present for what is being communicated. Make yourself available to the experiment. This is not the sort of thing to try when you have limited time or are in a hurry. If you want to go deep, try to include people who are not your typical partners for conversation. Attempt to include those with whom you might usually disagree, and also experiment with people you already love and think you know well, to see if you can discover something new about them or confirm what you've always thought about them.

Here are some questions to help you deepen your listening skills:

- What are they saying?
- What aren't they saying?
- What do they mean?
- What words does the speaker emphasize, and what does that tell me?
- What feelings do I detect behind the words being shared with me?

You may already know what it is like to talk to someone who doesn't give you their complete attention. Don't be like that. Instead, make an effort to be present. Don't interrupt the speaker, try to notice what they are feeling, and give your full attention to them while they are speaking.

The Compassion of Being There

How Compassion Means Being There for Others

"Being There" is the motto of the Law Enforcement Chaplaincy in Sonoma County, an interfaith organization that is a model of compassionate presence at death notifications, traffic accidents, suicides, and wherever peace officers call for support. To be effective, a chaplain in this organization must abandon all thought of proselytizing so that at times—such as when a natural disaster, loss, or grief strikes—they can show up with a clear focus on support and understanding. I trained to be a chaplain and the most valuable awareness I received from the training was that it is impossible to prepare a chaplain for every kind of situation where their services will be needed. Eventually, a chaplain has to trust their ordinary goodness to be a compass. They must let it guide them in how to be compassionately present when they don't know the right words to say to a grieving mother whose daughter just died in a car crash, or when they are exhausted from staying up all night with a traumatized family. Being there for other people, it turns out, has less to do with having the right words to say and more to do with respectfully witnessing another person's experience. It's not a new skill. Kent Nerburn describes the reverence the Lakota had for silence, which they preferred over talking as the practice of true politeness, writing that "in the midst of sorrow, sickness, death, or misfortune of any kind, and in the presence of the notable and great, silence was the mark of respect. More powerful than words was silence with the Lakota."*

I learned how to be quiet in traumatic situations and avoid contributing further harm by offering advice before it was welcomed or appropriate. I learned to trust ordinary goodness, not to make me feel comfortable, not necessarily to make a situation right, but to make me be there for the complex and intense situations I was called to serve in. Instead of focusing on the correct thing to say, and instead of trying to erase painful feelings, I let myself think about what goodness in the form of compassion would want me to do. I began to trust that it would inform me, not only in my role as a chaplain but in life also. When I consult compassion, it reliably informs me of my duty to contribute relief to the world's suffering, both materially and with my attitude. My attitude, I learned, plays a significant role in how effective a compassionate presence I would be as a chaplain. I had to learn to be both caring and courageous, and that if I was unprepared mentally as a chaplain, I could be a disruptive presence rather than a help. I think of it now in terms of maintaining an elevated consciousness and not letting my thoughts drag me down into inaction or apathy.

A chaplain, when on call, must be ready at any moment. In a meeting of local governance, a civic chaplain may similarly have to be prepared at a moment's notice to pray should the meeting become rowdy and require re-centering. To be prepared, such chaplains can't

* Kent Nerburn, ed., *The Wisdom of the Native Americans* (Novato, CA: New World Library, 1999), 9.

become embroiled in the discussions and emotionally entangled. If they do, their state of mind might not be conducive to prayer. Being a law enforcement chaplain taught me a similarly valuable lesson about being there for others—about being caring, but not collapsing emotionally into the details of the situation. Being present and clearheaded as a compassionate witness allows others to have their experience. Sometimes compassion will guide us to do something, and sometimes it will guide us to be something. I tend to place more value on action, and I have had to learn that being there can also be a valuable and compassionate contribution.

Compassion When You Can't Be There

When fires swept over Lake County, California, just north of my town, my thoughts, from time to time, would be hijacked by my fear for the people affected, for the first responders, and for those who lost entire homes. I would sometimes find myself stuck in downward-spiraling thoughts that had the effect of immobilizing me. I was frustrated to be so near to the disaster and not able to contribute. There were so many people engaged in responding to the event that the public was advised not to show up until the authorities requested assistance. It took an effort of will to extract myself from feeling ineffective and to redirect my attention to the extraordinary acts of human kindness that emerged during the disaster. But, I asked myself, was thinking about the goodness that was coming forward enough of a contribution?

A man went on a personal pilgrimage to India where he served in an ashram, feeding the poor and sick. He asked the guru of the ashram, who was serving food along with the rest of the devotees, how the guru felt about monks in more contemplative orders who sat in meditation and didn't do much to help the sick and poor. The guru said,

"Ah. If it were not for those monks and their practice, we might not be able to do the work that we do, for if we all abandon contemplation of wholeness, our work would have no foundation upon which to stand. It is necessary that each do what is theirs to do and not anything else."

I wanted to do something to contribute to the relief of those affected by the fires. And I wanted to do it in such a way that my attitude and emotional energy would be a valuable support and not add to the anxiety and fear already present. The first thing I had to attend to was what my mind was focusing on. I was feeling helpless and sad. Imagination is a powerful tool to use, and in the form of an optimistic vision of the future, it can inspire us not only to feel hopeful but to take appropriate action. Although I could not be part of the relief effort physically, I wanted to take heed of the guru's idea and believe that nurturing a good frame of mind would in some small way contribute also. The opportunity for those of us not physically involved was to become engaged in holding the high watch by using our imagination. I borrowed language from Centers for Spiritual Living's organizational vision to create my own series of statements to focus on and to inspire me to envision what the future might be:

- *I see Lake County as a place to practice generous and continuous sharing of heart and resources.*
- *I see Lake County free of homelessness, violence, and hunger.*
- *I see Lake County as a place in which forgiveness is the norm—whether for errors, injustices, or debts.*
- *I embrace a vision in which Lake County has renewed its emphasis on beauty, nature, and love through the resurgence of creativity, art, and aesthetics.*
- *I see Lake County as a place in which fellowship with all life prospers and connects through the guidance of spiritual wisdom.*

- *I envision Lake County as being an example of a place in which we live and grow as One Global Family, a place where there is respect and honor for the interconnectedness of all life.*
- *I see Lake County as a model community of inspired individuals caring for and about each other and the entire global family, thereby bringing the gift of active compassion and kindness to the world.*
- *I see the leaders of Lake County as points of inspiration and influence effectively demonstrating the power of ordinary goodness.*

Focusing on something beyond the crisis does not numb me or lull me into inaction. Rather it causes me to notice what good people are doing and inspires me to participate as I can. I began to see significant expressions of sharing, compassion, and assistance in the presence of tragedy and destruction. Our local credit union, Redwood Credit Union, facilitated a donation-collection program, carrying the administrative costs and legal fees to set up the account and giving 100 percent of donations to those affected by the fire. The credit union offered 0 percent loans to those in need of living expenses, car replacement, and the like. I donated. Donations in the first twenty-four hours exceeded the $100,000 goal.

Because I was inclined to use my imagination to raise my awareness, I set myself up to notice the things that good people do when bad things happen. I learned about awe-inspiring acts of openheartedness and sharing. For example, Ronald Wright, president at El Molino Boosters (an organization of parents and supporters of students at El Molino High School) helped to coordinate contributions for students of Middletown High School to help replace the sports gear that was destroyed by the fire. This helped them to look ahead and have faith in the future. Letitia Renee Hanke coordinated caravans of supplies and took pallets of donated food from Santa Rosa to the displaced in Lake County, and she used social media to help coordinate the logistics and let people know how and what they could donate.

Ordinary goodness, as I wrote in the opening of this book, is not dead. It's just ordinary. For it to become fascinating, the habit of not noticing it must be interrupted, and goodness must be cherished and enjoyed—resolutely and mindfully. Thinking about and paying attention to the ordinary compassionate acts of others can be inspiring and cause us to be more compassionate ourselves.

Practice
Imagine the Future

Thinking of a current challenging situation in your life, or in the world, take a moment to create a mental image of the situation sometime in the future when it is favorably resolved. Describe the imagined future in a series of short statements, beginning with "I see . . . ," as in the list given above. Or, if you prefer, express your imagined future in the form of a blessing, as in the example below from a Facebook status update:

> *I read an account yesterday of someone's experience of their evacuation from Harbin Hot Springs; they were the last ones to go. As they were leaving, she could see the fire arriving and the beginning of the loss and destruction that was possible. As she inwardly looked beyond what her eyes were showing her, she was filled with gratitude for what she had and described this wonder of witnessing God's glory and magnificence as fire. Its powerful dance left her in awe.*
>
> *It reminded me of New Year's Day in 1997 during the Napa River flood. My family lived near the river, and the rains had been relentless. Inch by inch, the water crawled up to our doorway and began entering our home, despite the fortress of sandbags we had*

placed before it. The idea of being displaced and witnessing this deluge I could not control was quite a struggle. At one point there came a sweet breeze of grace that took away this inner conflict. Not as a resignation but, like this woman who shared her story about the fire, I became intrigued by the magnitude of God's power showing up as this flood. Earth since time immemorial has been able to take care of herself, constantly creating new landscapes through the power of fire, water, wind, and earthquakes. That day I witnessed her strength. I too was filled with awe and wonder as the person who described the fire approaching.

Blessing: Today I bless all that have been affected by this fire, knowing that this has set a new course in motion for everyone. That what is now being birthed is greater and necessary for the evolution that is being called forth. I affirm that all are healed of their inner turmoil and open to the grace and blessings that this life event is offering. Out of destruction, new creation comes forth. Out of letting go of the old, there is receptivity to a greater fulfillment of purpose.[*]

Compassion When You're Trembling

The Greater Good Science Center—which studies psychology, sociology, and the neuroscience of well-being and teaches skills that foster a thriving, resilient, and compassionate society—states that doing something that alleviates suffering makes us feel good. Doing good leads to greater self-confidence, has positive health effects, causes us to be less vindictive, and makes us better parents, friends, and partners.[†] Compassionate people tend to be more

* Julie Schmidt, Facebook page. Used with permission.

† For a complete definition of compassion and the benefits of practicing cultivating it, see the website Greater Good: The Science of a Meaningful Life, http://greatergood.berkeley.edu/topic/compassion/definition.

socially adept, and those who avoid compassion may experience lower commitments to moral principles.

In the South African school system, primary school is the equivalent of American junior high. Education for white children during the apartheid era was government mandated and government subsidized. No matter how poor a white family was, the children attending school were assured to receive all their books and tuition at no cost. We didn't have long, extended summer breaks. Our breaks were equally spaced throughout the year and thus shorter than American school breaks. Sometimes our school organized excursions into the veld to learn about Africa's magnificent wilderness.* These school camping trips were thrilling. The wild veld is beautiful to witness, with wonderful smells and an environment that contains a paradoxical mix of profound, penetrating silence as well as the riveting sounds of nature. We didn't learn only about the wilderness at camp. In addition to basic survival techniques—what to eat, where to find water, this and that—we also learned that Creation had a plan for us white children of Africa. We learned that the Creator printed this plan in nature itself. The ranger told us so. He told us that it wasn't natural for people of different colors to commingle. It didn't happen between species in nature, and it shouldn't happen in society among people.

The flaw in logic prompted me to blurt out before I could stop my mouth and retract my raised hand: "But my grandfather raises parakeets . . ."

The ranger looked at me, his eyes defying me to continue along what was a clearly prohibited line of reasoning. The look on his face made me feel horrible. I was already considered to be an unusual child, and this questioning wasn't going to help me fit in.

---

* *Veld*, pronounced "felt," is the Afrikaans word for the open country of southern Africa's grasslands, characterized by shrubs and grass.

To some of my friends, I was that child with the Afrikaans name who couldn't speak the Afrikaans language any better than an Englishman. (I grew up in a mixed household in which more of my family spoke English than Afrikaans. Having an Afrikaans name and not being able to speak the language well, it turns out, was deeply offensive.) I was that child with the too-soft voice and the too-curly hair. I was the child with the big brown eyes and the flowery language, the boy who was fascinated with other boys. It felt like every set of eyes was watching me as I finished my wrong question. I imagined that they hated everything about me, and they couldn't hide it.

"My grandfather raises parakeets," I said again nervously, "and the blue ones mate with the yellow ones, and we can never tell what color the babies will be. Isn't that natural?"

My comment was met at first with silent tension. And then I was ridiculed by the rangers, who referred to my mixed heritage as the explanation for why I couldn't understand. After that morning, things at camp became unpleasant for me—nothing obvious, but I noticed that the rangers ignored me, and sadly, some of my fellow students did too. I was excluded from certain exercises, made to watch from the wings while others participated. When eventually I got home, I remember running from the bus to my father, who was waiting for me, and throwing myself into his arms and sobbing. I felt ashamed that I had caused trouble. I couldn't tell my mom and dad what had happened. I said instead that I had missed them and that I was glad to be home. At school, whenever I thought of camp, I began to feel anxious. I suppressed further comments about skin-color differences that might make me stand out from the other children even more than I already did. I became more nervous around them and began to notice what they were saying about my too-curly hair, my too-friendly attitude toward other boys, and my soft gentleness. I hadn't paid much attention to them before, but now their words seemed to jab at me uncomfortably. "Look at him," a boy who I thought was my good friend said to all the white boys sitting on the sidewalk waiting for the bus after school. By now, I knew what was coming and could feel the hot red flush of my cheek skin giving me away.

"He is half a girl and half black."

I didn't know what to do and didn't fully understand the meaning of his accusation. He spat out the words as if he were getting rid of a bite of rancid food, as if he had discovered something reprehensible and couldn't endure talking about it. I was confused. I was neither a girl nor black, but I understood that I was being accused of being something he detested. So I sat still fearfully and looked down, hoping my eyes would not betray me with tears.

"He lives in the slums," he added, as if to clarify exactly why he was so disgusted.

Apparently being white and poor at the same time somehow let down the whole white community. I didn't know that my family was poor. I didn't notice because I always had what I needed. I didn't know that wearing the same pair of shoes until I wore them out was a problem. I had to learn what poor meant, and I learned it at school from people like my accuser who seemed to find my existence intolerable.

"Look, he's crying."

I was about to flee, even though I knew that doing so would satisfy the bully and ensure that more harassment would come, when suddenly someone sat down next to me. He plopped down like a sack of potatoes and started talking to me as if nothing else was going on around us. I don't recall what we talked about, but I remember catching a glimpse of his hand shaking slightly. He was scared too, but not afraid enough to abandon me. I felt a powerful stirring of hope and gratitude because of his implicit recognition of my struggle. He would never know it, yet that act of solidarity not only saved me from a downward spiral into isolation, but it also planted a seed of courage in me that would prompt me to stand up for myself and others, even when I was afraid to do so.

Knowing that not everyone in school thought unkind thoughts about me was magical in its effect. It didn't work out in the most elegant way, and I'm not proud of how I fought back, but I did start to stand up for myself. I never cowered again. I never cried in front of them again. The ultimate turning point came when a group of senior boys gathered around me in the playground to taunt me. I was on my haunches playing with marbles in the sand. One of the taunters said, "Look how scared he is," and I realized that I wasn't really that scared at all, but they would continue to think so as long as I did nothing. So I stood up quickly and punched the leader of the bullies in the nose. It wasn't my finest hour, and I'm not proud of the event, and I don't advocate violence as a way of solving problems. I may have solved the immediate problem of bullying, but I earned a new reputation for being aggressive, and I could never shake the feeling of personal disappointment that I had struck someone as a way of solving a problem. After that, I stuck to myself mostly, but I was more inclined to stand up for the kids who were the underdogs on the playground. I didn't become fearless as a result of my reckless act of violence—I still shook with unease when I sat down next to someone like that boy had sat down next to me. I was still afraid to speak up and ask difficult questions—but the difference now was that I was more inclined to do what I had to do, even when I was shaking with fear.

Apologizing to the boy I hit wasn't an easy task. I had humiliated him, and he lost his status among his supporters. He would not talk to me. I could understand where he was coming from, but that didn't necessarily help me resolve my need to make amends.

The upside of the event was that I learned a little more about the complexity of being compassionate. I also learned that being there for someone doesn't require me to be confident or sure of the outcome. I learned that we can transfer hope to each other even when we are afraid.

Practice
Take Responsibility

In a class about spirituality, the teacher invited me to write a letter of apology to someone I had offended a long time ago through an unkind act. I had no idea where in the world the person was, or if they even remembered the event the way I did. The letter was not intended to be sent—rather, it was designed to help me get in contact with and own the feeling of regret. Before I wrote the letter, I hadn't taken the time to identify what feelings my memory of hurting another would evoke. Writing the letter helped me clarify my feelings and feel them. I had been afraid that if I tapped into the sense of regret, I would be overwhelmed with sadness and futility. In reality, the sadness was profound, but survivable, and apparently exactly what I needed to feel freer. The written acknowledgment of wrongdoing by me became a ceremonial act of admission. I have since then cherished working with a licensed therapist to review and confess painful memories. I consider my years in therapy to be among the most valuable contributions to my life because of the safe container therapy provides, one in which I can take responsibility for my actions and identify my feelings.

Reflect on times when you regretted your behavior or a choice you made. Think about what you might have preferred to do. Ask yourself what contributed to your decision and action. Imagine what might be different in your life had you chosen differently. Consider writing a letter to yourself or to the person(s) you may have offended. Keep in mind that the letter is for you and is not intended to be mailed. You might also consider burning or shredding the letter as a symbol of completion.

The Compassion of Caring About Others' Suffering

"Oh, that is terrible!"

Not only did my grandmother have a powerful conviction that everything works out in the end, but she was also able, paradoxically, to get into how terrible a thing was. It made her delightfully relatable. When I explained the details of some problematic situation, she would narrow down her gaze in concentration, as if peering over the top of her glasses at an especially troublesome insect on a table, and then click her tongue three times right before saying, "Oh, that is terrible," with stress on the word *terrible*. If it was a tough problem we were sharing with her, she would emphasize her empathy by saying, "Oh, that's just terrible, terrible, I'm telling you." Then, at the end of the conversation, she would wrap everything up with the familiar words "It will all work out in the end." It felt so good when she commiserated with us. It was like medicine to a traumatized soul. To have someone see us, hear us, and feel with us, whatever it was we were struggling with, validated our felt experience and gave us the courage necessary to face whatever was next. It didn't matter whether her assessment of our difficulty was accurate or not. The compassion of her witnessing, like the compassion of the boy who sat down with me, would give me and many others the fortitude to keep on going and work through our problems.

In the 1970s, I encountered the New Age idea that we are all ultimately responsible for everything that happens to us because of the creative nature of our thought. I found the idea intriguing, and I began to take responsibility for my life in a more attentive way. But I also began to miss my grandmother's empathic approach to life. She would never have asked the accusing question "What is in your thinking that created this situation?" Whether or not there is any truth in the notion that our thoughts create our reality, I found it utterly unhelpful in moments of intense struggles—when I was already hurting—to blame my thoughts. I responded better to compassion. Whether or not my consciousness is to blame for the problems in my life, compassion in the form of witnessing my struggles is the powerful remedy that empowers me the most. Of course, there is a relationship between my thinking and the events of my life, but not in the immature way I first understood it to be. It's more complicated than that. It's very difficult to trace an event back to a particular thought that caused it. We intersect with each other's lives—we inherit the beliefs of our family and culture, and we are subject to the thinking of the most prominent adults around us during our formative years.

I began to explore how my thinking was affecting my life. I wondered if I was the only person with such messed-up thinking, if I alone created chaos. I wondered if everyone around me was far more conscious and in command of the type of thoughts they permitted to pass through their minds. In reality, we're all in the same boat, trying to figure out the relationship between our inner lives and our experience. Nevertheless, I felt isolated sometimes because it seemed that no one was listening to me when I talked about my struggle. It seemed that others imagined I was asking for advice, and they gave it. But I wasn't. I realize now that all I needed was three clicks of the tongue and an acknowledgment that what I was going through was difficult. I already knew that my troubles were paradoxically terrible and not terrible at the same time, and that things would work out in the end, and that I had played a significant part in shaping the troubles. My grandmother had trained me. I just needed some fuel in the form of compassion to fill my tanks so that I could get on with the task of moving through it. What I wanted was the warmth of empathy, and I didn't know how to ask for it.

Now, if someone consults with me and they are in the middle of a journey through a dark place in their lives, my first inclination is to nod in acknowledgment that I am hearing what they are telling me about their experience. I invite them to start at the beginning of their story, to spare no details, to avoid trying to be high-minded, to take as much time as they want, and to tell me every last detail. Sometimes, in the middle of their story, I click my tongue and nod my head in acknowledgment that I have heard them. I can wait a long, long time to hear all they have to say. I can listen and not offer advice. This way, the people who come to me feel my grandmother's love expressing itself through me.

Thank you, Grandma.

I remember an especially challenging time as a young adult. I was sharing an apartment at the time, and when my roommate came home from work, he found me in a dismal state. My emotions were messy, and I felt sad and stuck. With good intentions, he began to offer me advice on how to cheer up and move through the sadness. He had suggestions for how to think correctly about it. I interrupted him. I was longing for connection. I thought it might be helpful to advocate for my needs and give him specific directions and suggestions of my own.

"John," I said, "I want you to respond like this. No matter what I say, you say, 'That's awful.' No matter how incorrect my perceptions may be, you only say, 'That's rough,' and then you nod to show you've heard me. Are you willing to try that?"

John was good-natured and kindhearted. He indulged me. I was able to pour my heart out, even though I knew he was humoring me. I stumbled through the stuck places and began to feel some relief because another being was being mindfully present for me. I appreciated his willingness to play along. It was a soothing experience for me. Later, he would tease me by answering cheerfully, "That's just awful," no matter whether the news I was sharing was good or bad.

In moments of struggle, people benefit from having someone hear their experience without necessarily saying anything at all. My growing sensitivity to this made me notice how many times I filled the space between another person and me with unsolicited advice. I began to practice being quieter and listening more. It helped me strengthen my role as a spiritual coach and gained me the reputation of being wise, ironically because I said so little. It was my grandmother's wisdom that produced these excellent results. When people came to see me who were in the middle of a painful event, I listened generously. I tried to keep in mind that they were likely to know more about their needs than anyone else does and that I was participating in witnessing their attempt to clear congested spaces in their lives. Sometimes if the situation they were sharing was particularly traumatic, or if it reminded me of some similar wounding in myself, I might feel myself slipping from empathic listening into assessing them, or preparing myself to offer advice even before they had finished speaking. In those moments, I would remind myself gently to return to listening to the person before me with a kindhearted interest.

This listening approach to sitting with others has been more beneficial and helpful than any other I have tried in communicating compassion. I abandon the goal of fixing people or offering advice. I forget about trying to make them feel better. I try to see them sitting before me exactly as they are, and I try to love them as my grandmother loved me. I try to hear truly and understand their suffering. And, as a by-product, I now know the powerful compassion that arises when I'm kind to myself in the same way.

The Compassion of Self-Kindness

When getting caught up in the lessons of honing our ordinary goodness toward others, it's easy to forget that it's just as important for us to apply that same kindness to ourselves. Learning to apply self-kindness in our own lives can create the experience of feeling safe and accepted by someone whose opinion we value: ourselves. We tend to have strong opinions about ourselves, and our internal conversations influence us perhaps more than any other person's—because, as Sally Kempton said, it is hard to fight an enemy who has outposts in your head.* We can be harsher with ourselves than we are with another person because we know ourselves so well and are familiar with our fears, hopes, and dreams. Undoing habits of self-criticism may not be comfortable, but it is worthwhile trying to undo them nonetheless.

Think about something that has troubled you recently because you were unsatisfied with how you handled the situation. Recall what your self-talk about it was like. If your thoughts are too fast

---

* Sally Kempton, "Cutting Loose," *Esquire*, July 1970.

or too jumbled, try writing down what you have been saying to yourself. Now try to imagine what a dear friend would say to you about your role in the situation. Imagine a friend who is kind, well-adjusted, and mature, and write down the response you believe he or she would give.

The point of the exercise is to notice that a friendlier self-talk may be possible and appropriate as a way of showing compassion to yourself. It may be necessary to pay attention to critical or angry self-talk and to interrupt it with a firm "Stop" inside your mind, followed up immediately with something a good friend might say. The irony is that these imagined words a good friend might say are likely to be more accurate about you and the situation than the words of your self-critical mind are, even though you know yourself best. Is it possible that you may have listened to the harsh kind of talk for so long that it seems truer because it is so familiar?

You may ask: What if I don't know any supportive, good types to use for this exercise? Then you will have to invent a person who is your advocate, who doesn't compare you to others, who sees how you try and acknowledges your effort. This person doesn't lead with advice or corrections but tends to point out your progress, causing you to feel understood and reminding you that you are valuable. Use this imaginary hero to make up what a kinder voice might say when commenting on your role in an unfortunate event.

It may take some training to stay on track with more considerate self-talk, because negative words have the habit of slipping back into place quickly. If you do slip, don't be mean to yourself about it; don't yell at yourself in your mind. Instead, pause and reassure yourself that it takes a long time to interrupt the activity of one's mind, especially if it is accustomed to running around out of control. The process of training self-kindness into your nature requires patience and firmness. Instead of mercilessly judging yourself for every transgression, imagined or real, focus on being kinder toward yourself—and to do this, you may be required to step in and stop an inner dialogue if it has a nasty tone. Being kind to yourself is a good place to start, and being compassionate toward yourself means going even a step further than kindness, to accepting yourself and all the voices that are in you, the kind ones and the cruel ones.

There are subtle differences between self-kindness, self-esteem, and self-compassion that are helpful to understand. Self-kindness is the practice of treating yourself decently, like a good person would, with gentleness and consideration. Self-esteem is feeling good about and thinking well about yourself based on skills, accomplishments, and appearances. Self-compassion, though, doesn't require achievements of any kind. Rather it grows out of the recognition that all beings are worthy of kindness—regardless of their struggle, their looks, or their success. In this way, self-compassion is the more valuable personal skill to develop, and the more rewarding one. Self-compassion understands that feeling good about someone or about yourself, based on conditional things like attainment or favorable comparison, is a pitfall—because when these things are gone, the positive self-esteem goes with them. Self-compassion embraces the whole person, just as they are and just as they are not. Self-compassion means being gentle with ourselves when things don't turn out the way we hoped, or when we have made a mistake or done something we regret. Self-compassion is not the same as obsessing about regrets—it is not self-pity or feeling angry because circumstances aren't what we want them to be. Self-compassion can be the act of giving ourselves an understanding break, even though we may have messed up.

A too-strict standard of perfection can get in the way of self-compassion, as does the idea that suffering is required before happiness can be deserved, or the notion that gentleness can only be given to those who earn it through hard work. We may withhold compassion from ourselves forever if we wait until we deserve it. Think instead of how we love infants. They do nothing to deserve our love. They don't earn it with words of affirmation, good listening skills, or reciprocation. They fall asleep when it's not convenient for us, and they wake up when it is convenient for them. They can be completely needy and sometimes high-maintenance. And yet we love them just the way they are. My cat is like that too. He disregards my plan to focus on work, and after he has eaten, he doesn't thank me but instead loses himself in an ecstatic dance with an empty paper bag. I watch him and think that he doesn't deserve any of that happiness, and yet he blatantly consumes it without ever having paid the rent, washed a dish, said something nice, or done anything that would earn him his place in the world. Can I extend some of that same unearned kindness to myself? If not, why not? Helping others is a beautiful way to express our ordinary goodness, but not as a way of earning self-compassion and kindness. There is a more compassionate way to treat ourselves—by not withholding kindness for any reason ever. When we completely believe in our ordinary goodness, we will be able to let ourselves enjoy life the way it ought to be appreciated.

But self-compassion and self-acceptance ought not to be confused with self-indulgent behaviors that disregard common sense or the well-being of others, or that succumb to destructive obsessions. Instead, self-compassion is the voice that recognizes the difficulty of walking away from a temptation, and self-compassion has no words of blame for those times when we don't walk away and feel that we capitulated.

Sometimes we fail, sometimes we fall, sometimes we fall short of the perfection we aspire to—and always we deserve compassion.

The Compassion of Seeing People as They Are

Do as I Say, Not as I Do!

My grandmother wasn't always saintly. She wasn't always mindful or perfect with her responses. Sometimes the thrill and the chase of the latest paperback novel she was reading would get the better of her, and she would become engrossed in its story and reluctant to tear herself away from her escape. She could be snippy with the kids she was babysitting if she had been captivated by some book. At such times, she would throw out instructions from over the rims of her glasses while barely moving her face or adjusting the position of the exciting book she held in one hand (and tea, of course, in the other). On one occasion, I remember I wanted to read a book rather than complete a chore. She insisted from behind her book that I do the chore, and I challenged her as to why it was okay for her to read the book and not for me to do the same—to which she responded: "Do as I say, not as I do."

Values are those qualities that an individual or society considers important as guides for conduct and that are fundamentally worthwhile. Along with politics, religion, freedom, and liberty, values can push buttons. I like to ask people what they value, and I like to explore why I, like my grandmother, frequently think that other people ought to observe my values even when I don't. The topic opens up the discussion about right and wrong.

I was indignant that my grandmother wouldn't budge from her opinion. I was frustrated that her instructions, unjust as they were, remained immovable. I learned from her that people don't always agree about right and just ideas and that, in the face of superior authority, I would have to learn to compromise. I learned the value of acknowledging that people may have different opinions, even irreconcilable differences, and I made a covenant with myself—one I would frequently break—to not foist my values on others.

I've told this story about my grandmother and her rule of "Do as I say" to friends who are parents. They acknowledge that creating rules about conduct with the explanation "Just because" or "Because I said so" often produces the opposite effect from the one they were hoping to achieve. People, it seems, need a little more than "Do as you're told" for an explanation, and don't respond well to "Because that's how it is." I went about my tasks with bitterness. I loved my grandmother, and she loved me, yet her behavior in this instance was unjust. I remember thinking, "I won't do this to anyone."

We can decide how to behave. We can become increasingly aware of what governs our actions, and in becoming aware, we start to understand what we value. In the process of observing what directs our choices, we may notice the role society plays (whether that is good or not), how strong the influence of the majority opinion is on us, and even the role the dominant adults in our formative years played. Then, through identifying and separating these strands of influence, we may begin to inquire into what central and profound convictions we have about life and goodness, faith and kindness—and decide to let them be an influential factor in how we move through this world.

It would have been ungenerous for me to characterize my grandmother's personality as dictatorial or unkind based on her obsession with paperback novels and her unjust (to me) treatment of the children in her care. In the bigger picture of her encounters with the people in her life, this minor weakness was more of a necessary color on a beautiful painting than it was a blemish. Nevertheless, I have also learned to value and learn from the actions in my life that come out of my moments of weakness. From time to time, I will hear people say, "I can't help myself" or "I am powerless to do differently." Now I know there are any number of unseen influences in the world. I am aware that not everything fits into a simple definition, yet I take to heart these words sometimes attributed to Gandhi:

Watch your thoughts; they become words.
Watch your words; they become actions.
Watch your actions; they become habits.
Watch your habits; they become your character.
*Watch your character; it becomes your destiny.**

I believe we have some freedom in these areas, and in that freedom lies the power to create havoc or harmony, to harm or to heal. In that freedom is an obligation to choose one behavior over another and to take responsibility for what we choose while being mindful of the wake our choices leave behind us.

---

* These words are sometimes attributed to Mahatma Gandhi and sometimes to Lao-Tzu. They appear in similar form in the Brihadaranyaka Upanishad (4.4.5) as "You are what your deep driving desire is. As your desire is, so is your will. As your will is, so is your deed. As your deed is, so is your destiny."

When I argued hard with my grandmother about what I would and wouldn't do, she'd sometimes say, "That's all very well, but you're not going to get away with it in the end." Back then, I didn't know what she meant by that, except that there seemed to be some vague threat in the words, and that in itself caused me to moderate my behavior. I'd explain to my grandmother that I didn't want to do a chore, and she would say, "Oh, I'd love to be able to do *only* what I want." She would say these things and not develop the argument or explain the meaning. I'd remember the utterances and wonder about them as an adult, and what they implied about personal freedom. Small imperfections set aside, my grandmother taught me what integrity means. To me, it means having a harmony between my behavior and my core beliefs a majority of the time. It is a condition of symmetry between my words and actions. It means that my words and actions reflect the same values.

I did learn from her example. Her restraint in not speaking when agitated or angry is among the treasured examples of conduct I integrated into my life. I learned more about her beliefs and values through watching her than through anything she ever said. I never was able to get her to talk about God, religion, values, or ethics, but she put her values on the table for all to see every day through her living. Thinking about her when I'm troubled, I remember more clearly the times when she comforted me than the times when she frustrated me. Remembering her love makes it easier for me to be compassionate to others. Remembering her quirks reminds me not to take myself too seriously.

For Crying Out Loud

Everyone has their limits. My grandmother had hers. There were times when she reached her capacity to be kindheartedly attentive to us. In those moments of exasperation, she would "tell it like it is," or at least her version of doing so. At moments when other people might say, "For God's sake," she might roar, "For crying out loud." Experience taught me what was coming next; she was going to lay down the law. She was about to tell me exactly what I was going to do, or stop doing, and exactly what was going to happen next if I didn't listen. I would brace myself because I knew better than to argue with her. I had no reason to fear her. She never hit me. Even as a young adult, when I was much taller than she was and she was frail and small, that voice continued to have the power to stop whatever madness was disturbing the home and to command respect.

I loved her even more during moments like those, perhaps because she was clear, direct, and easy to understand. I knew exactly what she meant and what she expected of me. Something was comforting about the clarity of her intent. I try to remember her speaking up in this way when it comes time for me to advocate for my needs. Although she was angry, she was not mean-spirited. She may have been disappointed or cross, but her words were easy to take in because she did not use anger. She did not put other people down or make them feel bad. She owned her anger, and instead of wielding it like a weapon, she used it to energize her communication and make her point. I remember her restraint—she would not succumb to using ugly words or mean expressions. I aspire to be like that in moments of difficult communications. Sometimes I am tempted to think that nasty words will make my point better than kindness. Sometimes I cry out silently, in my grandmother's voice, "For crying out loud," and it reminds me to abandon bad behavior as a way of expressing my needs. It gives me pause to let heated thinking cool down enough so I can find the more beautiful way to say whatever it is that needs to be said. More than anything, I remember my grandmother for her tolerance, not for her outbursts.

She had a way of allowing people to be who they were, while at the same time expressing what she needed. She gave me faith that people can reach across differences and coexist. Seeing people as they are and accepting them with kindness was something that I would ultimately have to learn to apply to myself also.

Practice

Remember the Love

Although many people may have hundreds of friends on social media, in reality one person can nurture about 150 meaningful connections, whether that is on social media or in real life. The theoretical limit of 150 friends has become known as Dunbar's Number after the British evolutionary psychologist Robin Dunbar, who reported the limit in the journal *Royal Society Open Science.** It appears that we have limited resources to commit to meaningful connections. We can either spread it thinly among many people or thickly among fewer people.

It's likely that a person has about five intimate friends, twice as many excellent friends, and about fifty very good friends. Beyond that, the people in our circles are likely acquaintances.

How well do you know the people in your circles? Who can you go to for compassionate support? Try this. Write down the names of people you can count on to help you when you are troubled. Then, next to their names, identify the qualities they show when they support you—for example, "good at listening," "caring," "supportive," etc. Look at the resulting list of qualities. Notice any recurring qualities or themes, as these are likely to be strong influences on you.

---

* http://www.dailymail.co.uk/wires/afp/article-3407569/Facebook-acquaintance-category-study.html.

PART FOUR

Ordinary Faith

We should be able to recognize true and perfect love by whether or not someone has great hope and confidence in God, for there is nothing that testifies more clearly to perfect love than trust.*

—*Meister Eckhart*

---

* Meister Eckhart, *Selected Writings* (New York: Penguin Books, 1994), 24.

Faith as an Expectation of Good

How Faith Is Taking the Risk to Believe Something That Cannot Be Proven

My grandmother had faith that all things work out in time. I realize now that it took great strength for her to proclaim that faith when life disproved it frequently. She would, nevertheless, resolutely declare that she expected good to come about, and then she would wait for things to work out as expected. An observer might not be able to tell what her religion was, but they would be able to tell that she had faith in something: an elegant rightness with the world. I admired her expectation of good, but I didn't always share it. Taking a risk to believe something without proof seemed reckless. I remember learning in Bible class that faith is what makes a person whole. I remember teachers repeating Jesus's words to the centurion—"It shall be done for you as you have believed"—as if they would be comforting. But Jesus's words did not give me the confidence they gave to the centurion. They distressed me. I worried that faith meant being able to believe in something utterly impossible.

On the one hand, I felt like Alice, who in *Through the Looking-*

Glass protested to the White Queen, "There's no use trying . . . one can't believe impossible things." On the other hand, I wanted to believe the Queen and felt encouraged when she answered, "I dare say you haven't had much practice. When I was your age, I always did it for half an hour a day. Why, sometimes I've believed as many as six impossible things before breakfast." Perhaps faith was a matter of practice and I could learn to stretch the boundaries of what I thought was possible or likely. I thought that if I leaned into it, I would finally get it.

Trusting God was altogether more challenging than trusting good, like my grandmother advised me to do, possibly because of what I had learned in school about God's personality. The ideas I learned about God presented insurmountable challenges for me. I could find no way to have faith in a God who has personal preferences when it comes to nationalities, or who is vengeful, wrathful, or jealous. These biblical descriptions of His temperament made me afraid. To trust that kind of God seemed utterly foolish. It made more sense to trust a vengeful person to be vengeful and a jealous person to be jealous, in the same way that we trust a chair to be a chair. My colleague Chris Michaels, author of *The Power of You*, said in a public address, "For us to progress as a people and create a more peaceful world, we have to give up the idea of a regional god with personal preferences. He is primitive and outdated." I turned my attempts to trust God into an attempt to expand my expectation of good.

Developing Expectations of Good

To me, faith and trust are connected through experience. I reframe statements such as "I have no faith in that" to "I have no experience of that." If someone presents a challenge of faith to me—say, for example, in the exaggerated statement "Just believe your amputated leg will grow back"—I respond with "I have no experience of that." This has helped me tremendously because now my goal is to broaden my experiences so that my expectations grow also. I thought this would be the way to increase my faith. Surely the time would come when I would be able to have faith in something that couldn't be proven. After all, that is how my grandmother came to be so certain. By watching how life unfolded, she accumulated evidence and became confident in predicting something she could trust—that everything works out.

That's the approach I took to expand my expectation of good. I tried to accumulate evidence that supported my point of view. Do I feel better with a regular practice of sitting in meditation? Yes. Am I capable of more generosity of spirit when I regularly foster an attitude of loving-kindness? Yes. The answers to questions such as these helped me speak with more frankness and confidence about the experiences that lead me to greater expectations of good. When I taught people to practice themselves, I wasn't asking them to believe in anything impossible and unproven. I was inviting them to discover something I had discovered for myself. Nevertheless, because they had not yet experienced the outcome of practicing meditation, generosity, selfless service, or the like, they had to accept the invitation on trust. They couldn't know if what I was telling them was real or not until they practiced themselves. There are times in life when we trust before we have evidence to support moving forward, and if we always wait for adequate proof that we are going to be okay, we might not make any progress at all. I don't know why sometimes I feel confident taking a leap into the unknown. My gut feelings are part of it. Another part of it is the confidence I gather from other people who have traveled ahead of me and tell me what to expect. We can be inspired by those around us to take the first step. I wish my grandmother were around so that I could tell her how much she shaped my mind and inspired me to trust in what I couldn't prove.

Other people's courage inspires me. I am inspired when other people believe in me, particularly when I can't believe in myself. I am encouraged when others see something good in me that I can't yet see in myself. This may be why some faith traditions emphasize the value of keeping spiritual company and participating in conversations that encourage us and bring balance to the negative influences laid upon us in life. We clearly have remarkable power to influence each other. Think of how valuable the clout of word of mouth is to moviemakers when it comes to advertising movies. They know that you and I are more likely to see a movie if a friend tells us that it is good than if a well-crafted advertisement tells us it is good. We have more faith in people's testimony because it is based on their experience. I'm more likely to believe you if you see something good in me than if I have to look for it myself. Now, I'm not saying we should always base our estimation of ourselves or make life decisions on what others say, at least not entirely. I am saying that the company I keep makes a difference. There were times when my grandmother's words of affirmation provided the fuel I needed to take action. I may have felt insecure and had no experience to trust what I was about to do, yet I went ahead, not fully believing in the goodness and strength she saw in me—but because she saw it, I trusted her.

The quality of the conversations I am having has the same effect on me. Do my conversations with others inspire me to greater expectations of good? If not, I make adjustments so that I talk more with people who are interested in hope, courage, and goodness, and the atmosphere of the conversations I have regularly tends to linger with me. It affects my mood and my energy. I believe that a little bit of the energy from those we hang out with lingers with us in our memory and affects what we expect from life. That's why I am of the opinion that faith can be absorbed by being near those who have a lot of it. It's for that reason that I liked hanging out around my grandmother.

Out on a Limb

Here is a story that illustrates faith beautifully. A tightrope walker demonstrates to a crowd that he can walk on a rope stretched across a canyon. When he returns to the spectators, he asks, "Do you believe I can walk across the rope?"

"Yes," they reply.

Then he takes a wheelbarrow and walks across the rope pushing it ahead of him carefully to the other side and back. When he returns he asks the delighted crowd, "Do you believe I can walk across the rope pushing a wheelbarrow ahead of me?"

"Yes," they exclaim with growing excitement.

Then he puts a friend in the wheelbarrow, and to the crowd's amazement and enjoyment, he conveys the friend safely across the canyon and back on the rope.

The tightrope walker asks the crowd, "Now, who would like to climb in the wheelbarrow and let me carry them across the rope?"

No one answers.

Variations of the story are told to illustrate the difference between belief and faith. It is a good story for that purpose, because even though I may have watched a tightrope walker complete the journey several times across the canyon, there remains a gap between my observation and my experience of it. It is the gap that is so fascinating. It's the gap that people are talking about when they say they went "out on a limb." I can't know if I'm going to make it safely across as the next passenger in the wheelbarrow. That's the gap. I think it's healthy and sane to be up front about the unknown element. I may decide to climb into the wheelbarrows of life, and when I make that decision, I may be trembling. When I do climb in, I'm not going to be counting on a primitive, regional god with personal preferences who is vengeful and jealous to make it all work out right in the end. If I fall, it's not because life rejected me or because I was bad or didn't have faith. If I fall, it's because sometimes people fall.

There is a risk.

I trust goodness in the form of the people who help me get up when I do fall. I don't trust a god who is like a superintendent watching over things, with a sort of random favoritism. If anything, I think of goodness as the intelligence that binds all existence together. I think of it as being present everywhere, in me and all people. I'm learning to be more aware of it and to draw upon it to figure out when I should get into a wheelbarrow and when I should not. To have that kind of relationship takes intimacy. In a relationship, trust and intimacy come with time spent together. I have been exploring an answer to the following questions: What does spending time with goodness—or with "God," if you prefer—mean? In its simplest form, it means the enjoyable practice of purposefully paying attention to the goodness in your life and noticing what's going on in your mind that distracts you from noticing goodness. What, you may ask, has that got to do with God? Well, when the mind is filled up with surface noise and commentary about events, remembered conversations, or imagined futures, it will be so noisy in there that there is not much room for anything else. When I pay attention to what I'm thinking, my mind tends to quiet down. Something about being an observer of my mind's activities is calming and lets me notice that there is quietness in me that has always been present. I call it wisdom, goodness, or inner peace. Others may call it God. It is sometimes blocked out by the noise of unsupervised thinking. When I spend time with inner peace, I become confident listening to what it is prompting me to do. Even so, I still encounter the gap between knowing what to do about the wheelbarrow and the other side of the canyon I want to reach. I may still encounter some doubt. This is natural enough, and because I have been practicing being quiet, I have become better at moving forward with a decision, even while experiencing some doubt or anxiety about it. When we access the quiet inside and become a frequent visitor to its abode, we will likely experience an increase in our ability to meet life's celebrations and challenges with understanding, more confidence, bravery, and levelheadedness.

I heard a speaker once invite his audience to train themselves to have high expectations of goodness. He was talking about building faith by expecting good things to happen. I came away from that upbeat message with a renewed commitment to living life as if it were good. I remember my grandmother's question again—"What good does it do to complain?" She would be tireless in looking for something good, and when she found it, she would say, "There you go," as if to explain that things were in the right place and all was well. It was as if she had made a promise to live life as if it were a good thing. She seemed fully aware of the strength it took to act accordingly, and expectantly, and it seemed impossible to thwart her appetite for cheering on good things.

Maybe faith is all about developing that kind of expectancy, or an affirmative attitude toward life. Maybe faith is something you have to work out for yourself; you may have to begin doing so by discovering what it is you do have faith in or what you're going to risk having faith in. Nobody can work this out for us, but we can encourage each other. My grandmother's encouragement was invaluable, and she continues to be inspiring to me years after her passing. The ultimate challenge with faith is that there is no insurance policy. The phrase "Love is blind" illustrates this because love ultimately cannot be reliably proven to exist between two people. There is a gap between what is knowable and what is not. I call that faith. Christian Larson describes the difference between hope and faith as the difference between standing still and taking action:

> *There is an abundance of hope in the world, but what we need is more faith. Everybody is hoping for better things. The poor hope to get rich. The sick hope to get well. The sad hope to gain happiness. The troubled hope to find peace. Everybody is hoping for something, but few have the faith that is necessary to secure that something. When we are in bondage, or keenly realize our bondage, we hope that the great Deliverer will come. We pray that God may come. We hope that our prayers will be answered, and we are so absorbed in our hopes that we fail to hear God knocking at the door even now. To have hope is to face the door. But hope stands still. It never moves toward the door. To live in hope is simply to face the great goal, but we may continue to face that goal for ages and never move forward a step. "To live in hope is to die in despair," because hope remains stationary. It never gains what it hopes to gain. But when faith begins, we remain stationary no more. We press on directly and with power toward the coveted goal. Our hopes are soon realized. Our desires are granted. What we wished for is withheld no more. Through faith, we have entered that world where every prayer is answered and every wish made true.*[*]

At some point when choosing a partner, we have to take action without full knowledge of the future. We have to reach over the

---

* Christian Larson, *The Pathway of Roses: Updated and Gender-Neutral* (Chicago: Newt List, 2015), 132.

gap between not knowing and making a decision to trust someone with our hearts. There is no method to prove their love, and without stepping out onto the skinny branch, love can't flourish. Questions I ask myself on those skinny-branch moments include: Is this a head trip, or have I spent sufficient time in my quiet mind to know that this is a faith trip? Call it a heart trip if you like. I've learned, during skinny-branch moments, to press the imaginary pause button—in other words, to refrain from quick responses, knee-jerk reactions, and impulse decisions (which I call a head trip), so that I can take a moment to breathe and think about what faith is prompting me to do.

If I have more fear than faith, it may not be the right time for me to step out on the skinny branch. I have made many mistakes by stepping out thinking my faith would arrive, all while my heart was saying gently to me, "Not yet." I have had to learn to follow more than my head's prompting and to take into consideration the bigger picture. Sometimes it is my heart that says, "It's skinny-branch time," and that is the time when I have had the experience of the road rising to meet my every step when I start the journey.

Practice
What Do I Think About?

Taking time daily to sit quietly and observe your mind is called meditation. At first, it was difficult for me to meditate, as it is for many people. The idea that we are supposed to clear our minds of all thought and have an emptiness in our heads made the task seem impossible. When I began meditating, I would become anxious because, instead of quieting down, my mind got busier with thinking. A friend advised me to stop trying to do anything at all. Instead of attempting to banish thoughts that appeared in my mind, I was to follow them. I worried that some of the thoughts were negative and obsessive and that they would disrupt my inner quiet. But over time, I learned that, just as my friend predicted, I would become an impartial observer of my thinking.

Some people also use the technique of mentally talking to the thoughts that pass through their minds. They might pretend that each thought is a person and ask it, "What do you want me to know?" Approaching meditation this way helped relieve the anxiety that arose when I became aware of how crowded with thoughts my mind was. Instead of trying to wrestle my mind into submission, I dropped expectations of how it should be and found my quiet mind was available even in the presence of all the mental noise. I began to notice a foundation of quietness in me and began to become more interested in the quietness than in the noise. Maybe it is because I stopped resisting what was in my mind. A teacher once said to me that thoughts are like independent beings, and when I threaten their existence, they are likely to fight back for survival. I've never forgotten that image, and I use it now when I feel frustrated about the content of my mind. Instead of fighting my thoughts, I treat my mind with more understanding, and if it is troubled and busy and scary in there, I don't run away—I sit and take a deep breath and look in at everything that is inside. I call that meditation because when I get up from this exercise, I feel more peaceful and have a more understanding attitude toward myself, and a bigger-picture view of life. I call that peace of mind.

For more information on the practice and power of meditation, check out my book *The Power of Meditation: An Ancient Technique to Access Your Inner Power.*

Faith as Something Borrowed

How to Borrow Faith When You Don't Have It

Where do you get faith when you don't have it? We can borrow faith from others who already have it. Prayer partners, best friends, grandmothers, and support groups, for example, are places from which we can borrow faith. A better way of saying it is that we can absorb faith by spending time with or being near people who are faith-filled. I think of it as "faith by osmosis." When I hang out with people who expect good, who believe that life is good, and who believe that reality is one big conspiracy for good, I begin to pick up their attitude myself. The atmosphere of their attitudes hangs around me after I leave their presence.

This reminds me of the Three Jewels of Buddhism: first, to take refuge in the Buddha; second, to seek refuge in the Teachings; and third, to seek refuge in the Sangha (the community of those who have attained a certain awareness and may help someone who is practicing achieve the same). Several years ago, I attended an ongoing education conference for ministers. The intention of the conference was to help ministers currently in pulpits expand beyond mental models of how ministry is supposed to be, so that they could thrive in their ministry and not merely cope with the duties heaped upon them. Among the many gems I took away from the conference was the question "What does your perfect day in the ministry look like?" I had never been asked that and realized I didn't know the answer. The follow-up question was ". . . and what gets in the way of your having that kind of day?" In response, one participant explained how she became bogged down by the drudgery and heaviness of dealing with demanding personalities who made it difficult for her to meet the needs of her job. The presenter asked, "Who in your community do you enjoy being with, and when last did you go out to have a cup of coffee with that person for a regular conversation?"

My colleague answered, "There hasn't been time."

What came out of the discussion was that my colleague was giving the majority of her time and energy to interactions that left her feeling drained. Listening to her, I remembered the sayings "Practice letting your conversations be more in heaven and less in hell" and "The squeaky wheel gets the grease." It became apparent to us how important it is to give priority time and space to the people we love, and to give them access to us so that their values and friendship can influence us. When we thought about the people in our ministries and in our circle of friends whom we loved and enjoyed, it became evident to us that we were likely to listen to their advice, encouragement, and insights. However, the problem was that these people were having an increasingly difficult time getting to us because attending to difficult situations and people was using up so much of our available time.

When I focus entirely on problems, I have the tendency to withdraw from my community—which is exactly the opposite of what helps me. When I withdraw from others and have to depend entirely on my own resources to solve life's problems, I lose contact with my faith. You may know what it is like to have no faith and still have to make choices and decisions. I do. I remember when the organization I work for purchased an old roller rink to convert into a spiritual community center. At the time, I thought the project was too big a stretch for me to manage. I wondered if I should quit and make way for a CEO with more experience to spearhead the project. At times, it felt like I couldn't breathe, and my thoughts seemed to say, "This isn't going to turn out well." Fortunately for me, my lack of faith was not shared by the people around me, who had a clear vision of what could happen. Being surrounded by a community of excited, hopeful, and energetic people slowly but steadily lifted my spirits. Not all of the worst-case scenarios my pessimism was producing came to pass. And when things didn't work out well, the overall attitude of excitement and forward movement made it easier for us to correct course and keep going.

This is how I know I'm having a crisis of faith: I begin to look for the evidence of why things are going to fail. I begin to explore the worst-case scenario and work through it in detail in my mind and also in conversations with others. When I am talking about it, my voice takes on a tone of urgency and warning. If I notice this is happening, I take it as a sign that it is time to get out of my rut and hang out with friends who will remind me that I know better, even though guarantees are not available. That's what I mean by borrowing faith. It is one of the reasons spiritual community is so important to me. The interactions with other community members feed me. We take turns at being strong for each other.

Having Faith in the Worst-Case Scenario

Someone once said that worry was a negative use of faith. The statement made me think about how much energy I put into thinking about worst-case scenarios as if I trust them to come about more than I trust goodness to happen. Thomas Jefferson wrote to John Adams and addressed the topic of projected misfortunes:

> *You ask, if I would agree to live my 70, or rather 73, years over again? To which I say, yea. I think with you, that it is a good world on the whole; that it has been framed on a principle of benevolence, and more pleasure than pain dealt out to us.*
>
> *There are, indeed, (who might say nay) gloomy and hypochondriac minds, inhabitants of diseased bodies, disgusted with the present, and despairing of the future; always counting that the worst will happen, because it may happen. To these I say, how much pain have cost us the evils which have never happened! My temperament is sanguine. I steer my bark with Hope in the head, leaving Fear astern.**

Worry, when left unattended, can cause an imagined event to consume my thinking and interfere with my ability to be present. It can affect my emotions and the way I interact with others. The Bible (Matthew 6:34) advises us not to worry about tomorrow because it will take care of itself and each day has enough trouble of its own. The idea is that what we look for, we tend to notice. Someone called it "cocktail party awareness," referring to our ability to focus on a person talking to us in the midst of a noisy social setting; we can blot out everything else happening and be consumed with the conversation. If the conversation we are consumed with is focused on imagining the worst-case scenario, it may be well to take into consideration Martin Tupper's words from 1839, which suggest that many of the worst-case scenarios we imagine in fact never happen:

---

* Thomas Jefferson to John Adams, April 8, 1816, Founders Online, National Archives, http://founders.archives.gov/documents/Jefferson/03-09-02-0446.

Thou hast seen many sorrows, travel-stained pilgrim of the world,
But that which hath vexed thee most, hath been the looking for evil;
And though calamities have crossed thee, and misery been heaped on thy head,
*Yet ills that never happened, have chiefly made thee wretched.**

* Martin Farquhar Tupper, *Proverbial Philosophy: A Book of Thoughts and Arguments, Originally Treated*, 3rd ed. (London: Joseph Rickerby, 1839), 27.

Finding Faith When There's Nothing Left Inside

How Surrender Is Not the Same as Giving Up

I remember a summer some years ago for its difficult clumping together of very painful events during one week. A member of our spiritual community drowned while snorkeling. A young person in our town walked onto the freeway in the middle of the night and was killed instantly. Two friends each lost beloved pets unexpectedly. Someone threw a rock through my office window, and another someone carved a swastika into the sidewalk outside our building. An acquaintance's son attempted to kill himself. By the end of the week, I felt unusually tired and empty. I have known for some time that cleaning house has the effect of calming frayed nerves, so I set about tidying a bookshelf. A greeting card dropped out of one of the books. The card announced on the front:

Things to do today—inhale / exhale.

The thoughtfulness of the person who sent the card had touched me, and I kept the card in the way I save inspiring bits and pieces of writing that come my way. I tuck them into the pages of favorite books so that I may stumble upon them in random moments, in moments like the one I found myself struggling through. The card had fallen from the book *Spiritual Economics* by Eric Butterworth. I had placed it near a well-loved passage from which I had often received encouragement:

> *It is an important moment in our lives, when we discover for ourselves the great Truth, that things may happen around us, things may happen to us, but the only things that really count are the things that happen in us. You may have precious little control of the elements or the fluctuation of the stock market or the unpredictable behavior of people. However, you live in a world of your consciousness, which is the sum total of the thoughts of your mind. You can control what goes on in your mind. This is not to say that it is easy but to establish that it is possible.**

The comfort I was expecting to come from the familiar words didn't show up. As I read the passage, the opposite seemed truer, that in fact I have absolutely no control over anything. I felt suddenly annoyed by the overly positive tone of the writing and the assertion that I could control what was passing through my thoughts and emotions. When we experience events that cause grief and sadness, we may feel the desire to retreat from cheerfulness, and it may be appropriate to do so for a time while we recover our sense of equilibrium. Grief is a normal part of being human,

* Eric Butterworth, *Spiritual Economics* (Unity Village, MO: Unity Books, 2001).

and sharing our pain with each other can help us get through it, without covering it over with positive thinking. There is a time for positivity, and there are times when it is inappropriate, at least in its form of forced cheerfulness.

A colleague of mine who served as a chaplain in a local police department worked closely with the coroner. He would be called out to assist in making difficult death notifications to families. On one such night, he received the call to attend to a death from sudden infant death syndrome, an especially tragic situation in which a child dies for no apparent reason. In the awkwardness of dealing with a long list of official questions, the young mother, supported by her husband, held their child as if holding on for a miracle to happen, for their baby to come back as suddenly as he had gone. Neither the coroner nor any of the officers at the scene wanted to interrupt the parents' vigil to remove their baby. Nevertheless, something had to happen, and the coroner looked to the chaplain for support.

The chaplain took a deep breath and said as kindly as he could, trying to erase some of the finality of the words, "It's time," and gestured to the waiting coroner. The young couple looked up with resentment at the thought of giving up their boy to this stranger. Then everything changed when the coroner gently took up the baby's body and did something unusual. He held the lifeless boy and rocked him tenderly in his arms, saying, "I want you to know that I will treat him as if he were my son."

Sometimes, when things get rough in life, I forget the incredible power of ordinary goodness and its ability to make a beneficial impact on the world. Sometimes grief and sadness drain our energy, leaving us with nothing to invest in the present moment. But we can be kind even when we are tremendously sad. There remains in us the power of ordinary goodness that we can draw upon to do something simple that shows our caring and that will communicate compassion and understanding, even when all is lost. The ordinary goodness demonstrated by the coroner inspires me. Its power is nothing fancier than plain decency. No special training is required to use ordinary decency, no special techniques. It can be messy, uncomfortable, and difficult. But we can trust it.

It's like the time in my mid-twenties when I worked in a health-food café as a waiter and served a lady with cerebral palsy. She wasn't expecting that the pineapple salad she ordered would come served in a half pineapple, balancing precariously on an empty plate. It slid on the plate beyond the ability of her one good hand to manage. In her attempt to have lunch, she launched raisins and lettuce all over the table in a café that was becoming increasingly awkward in its silence. I didn't know what to do, but I wasn't going to be the paralyzed-by-fear nineteen-year-old obedient soldier who sat by and witnessed brutality on a train again. At this moment, there was no threat of violence if I did nothing. Nevertheless, to me, the situation represented a milestone of courage. I sat myself down awkwardly next to her and asked if she needed help. She nodded, and I took that to mean to help her to eat. So I grabbed her spoon with the relief that comes with being able to do something to help and began presenting mouthfuls of delicious pineapple salad to her, which, it turns out, is precisely what she didn't want. She wanted the meal wrapped to go and needed extra time to explain what kind of help she needed. But I was in too much of a hurry to make myself feel better. Eventually, she managed to blurt out "Stop." I could feel my cheeks burning with the realization of what had happened. I had made things much, much worse.

Then it was her time to shine; keeping her hand on mine, she managed a smile, one that seemed to soften the moment and even to calm all of her struggling muscles so that they could obey her will.

"It's okay."

Her kindness washed over me, and we both cried. Straightforward kindness is one of the most beautiful forms of ordinary goodness I know. I remember these stories when things get dark. I try to remember them if I can, unless my thoughts become too constricted with sadness and empty me. The coroner, the lady in the café, and countless others remind me that ordinary goodness is simply the attitude with which I embrace life. Ordinary goodness, I've learned, *is* my spirituality, and doesn't have to have anything to do with a particular religion or spiritual practice. It has to do with caring. It has to do with the willingness to act upon caring even when I'm empty, even when I may not know the best, most elegant way to express it: it is the capacity to be kind and to have faith in that kindness, even when I'm not cheerful or in control of my thoughts or emotions.

Tripping on Positivity

The difference between easy positive thinking and what the coroner said to the parents of the dead infant is the genuine tenderness in an epically tragic event of human life. He did more to prove the perfection of life and the power of love at that moment than any wise teacher or sacred text ever has for me. To say something beautiful and tender at heartbreaking moments takes courage and understanding. I shy away from overly positive aphorisms that advise us to pick ourselves up, brush ourselves off, and start all over again. I find them to be too simplistic and, frankly, annoying. I remember when my favorite little blue car was stolen. In the grand scheme of things, it was a minor setback. But to my heart and mind this was a horrible, personal attack that left me angry and feeling victimized. I was so angry that I did not want to look for the silver lining—I didn't care if there was a disguised blessing, and I certainly didn't want to have any well-meaning friends explain to me how perfectly life was playing out for me.

Nevertheless, and as much as I don't like to admit it, I have also been rescued by genuine kindness in the form of cheerful and positive encouragement. I was running in a national park down a steep path on a trail well known for trips and falls. I tripped and fell. I sprawled ungracefully quite a bit ahead of an elite group of military types who were clearly in perfect physical shape. The graze on my knee was painful. The last place in the world I wanted to be was facedown in the dirt in front of the exact type of men who used to beat me up in school, just when I was getting fit enough to hold my own. I felt the sting of embarrassment on my cheeks, and to my horror, my eyes were tearing up uncontrollably. The leader of the pack arrived several moments ahead of his mates and stopped to help me. He picked me up like I was no more than a bag of groceries, looked into my face, and said, "Get up. You're okay. Don't let them see you cry, bud. You're doing great." He patted me on the back and sent me on my way down the hill again. To my surprise, I felt a surge of encouragement well up in me and became capable of doing anything. There was a time when I searched for goodness through God. I asked, along with so many people, why God doesn't show up when most needed. I paid attention during my meditation and prayer time, looking for answers. I have felt defeated when I received none. I think I wasn't paying attention to the right things. I wasn't noticing goodness showing up in ordinary ways. I was looking for supernatural intervention, and all the while I was missing the magical intervention of being picked up, brushed off, and sent on my way.

Practice

Thank My Way Out

Some simple practices can help me recover from life's weariness if I can remember to do them when I think I can't take any more. I turn my emptiness into gratitude by silently thanking everyone I contact. I don't make a big deal out of the exercise, and I don't tell anyone I'm doing it. I refocus my tired awareness on appreciating whatever I can. If I see someone helping a child, I say "Thank you" silently. If I see someone smiling at a friend, I say "Thank you" silently. If I keep at it, something moves in me. Nothing momentous happens. Life doesn't suddenly make more sense. The reasons for sudden infant death don't become clearer. But a slow warmth, like an inner light, begins to burn in me, and I begin to remember the gentle power of ordinary goodness. This is what it means to me to control my mind: to gently guide it back to goodness when I feel desolate, or when there seem to be no real options. Gratitude, when I have the strength and willingness to practice it, nudges me to notice things that are heartwarming and encouraging.

Wisdom Writings

Try this: make greeting cards with inspiring words from texts that you love. It is a beautiful act of sharing your passion and, in my opinion, conveys something more intimate and personal than purchasing a card with a pre-printed message. A friend complained to me that her handwriting was too untidy. I showed her a greeting card that I cherished and had kept for a long time. The handwriting was difficult to decipher because the writer had suffered brain damage from an auto accident. Nevertheless, the meaning and love the card carried have stayed with me and touched me enough that I have kept the card with my most cherished items.

I sometimes make hand copies of texts that inspire me because rewriting them in longhand is a slow and mindful exercise. It allows the text to sink into my memory. I am in the process of hand copying the Bhagavad Gita, one of the books I find the most inspiring. Now and then I open the Gita next to my blank journal and write a few verses. It is a meditative practice and a reminder that small things, like handwriting, are both wonders of being human and also something to be valued. Consider doing the same with a text you love, especially a text that focuses your attention on goodness. Consult the appendix for further resources on wisdom writings that may be suitable for this exercise.

I have collected stirring pieces, books, and hand-copied notes. I read them from time to time when my attention is distracted or when my focus strays from what is good and enduring. I have made the habit of gifting favorite pieces to others as a way of sharing the goodness I derive from the writings.

Faith as Something Earned

How Faith, Like Kindness, Is a Muscle That Must Be Exercised

There come times when I have to get in a wheelbarrow, and I know I am going to, and I have little or no evidence that doing so will be safe or advisable. Surviving these moments is one of the ways I accumulate faith. I call that earned faith, the conviction that comes from taking risks and stepping in the direction I'm being called to go, even while I am apprehensive about doing so. In this regard, faith is like a muscle that must be exercised and kept in good condition for it to perform well. Don't wait for the big challenges to come along before you exercise your faith. Practice during the good times as well. You can do that by giving people the benefit of the doubt, by trusting in goodness when there isn't a lot of evidence that you should, and by beginning to pay attention to your inner wisdom. Another way of earning faith is by making a habit of thinking about what is important to you and rededicating yourself to it.

Consider this "New Pledge of Allegiance," which was written by my colleague Dr. David Ault:

I pledge allegiance to breaking the self-imposed barriers of my humanness. I recognize that my time on this planet is precious and limited. Every day is a canvas on which I can create. Every day is an opportunity for me to move in the direction of the dreams and the expanded vision I feel inside. By setting aside petty grievances, past mistakes, righteous anger, and my broken story, I pledge to move forward and embrace the experience of freedom right here and right now.

I pledge allegiance to the expression of my spiritual honesty. I fully own the fact that my presence here in this body and on this earth is a celebration of uniqueness and importance. Creation makes no mistakes. I am a creation of life, of a higher power, of perfection. My reason for being here matters in the grand divine plan. I must be honest with my contract of life and walk the path of my destiny with conviction, purpose, and grace.

I pledge allegiance to the quiet soldier within. I understand that the championing spirit that is already cellularly alive inside of me, that was already in place at the time of my birth, waits patiently for my current belief about myself to join it in its knowing. I march forward toward a history of my own making, wisely, lovingly choosing the means by which I spread my beliefs and convictions. I never make others wrong for their chosen path, for I recognize the innumerable roads that lead to the One.

I pledge allegiance to a partnership with divinity. I choose to see others and myself from eyes that already view the wholeness and perfection within. I do not entertain our past damage or encourage us to identify with it, for I trust that a grander calling card has been printed for us to distribute in promoting our lives. I champion all of us to celebrate what is working rather than what isn't.

I pledge allegiance to wise discernment—knowing when to speak and when to remain quiet, knowing when to comfort and when to leave alone, knowing when to intervene and when to avoid rescuing and interfering.

I pledge allegiance to people and projects of substance. I cannot travel this road alone. If there is anything we as a species need, it is each other. I actively choose to support those whose work I believe in with my time, talent, and treasure. I joyously give to those whose intention and purpose is for self-empowerment and the awakening of humanity to its personal magnificence. I rally to make others aware of such light bearers and do what I can to support them in furthering their vision.

I pledge allegiance to the freedom from comparison. I once and for all lay down my wearisome, stale beliefs of unworthiness and not being good enough. I know that my past does not define who I am. I am forever evolving, growing, and learning. I recognize that I am a marvel. I now choose opportunities to let my voice be heard, to let my light shatter the darkness of futility so that every personal dream is explored.

I pledge allegiance in knowing that things are not always as they seem. Just because something can't be seen with the physical eye or rationalized by our current mode of understanding does not negate its existence. Understanding the difference between reality and illusion, I move into a fuller acceptance of the non-physical—the mystical, intuitive, soul aspect of living that expands my consciousness and deepens my days.

I pledge allegiance to actions that fulfill the greatest good for all. By becoming a gatekeeper of compassion, tolerance, and love, I move into a fuller conviction of pure intent with regard to the words that I speak and the choices that I make. I pursue a win-win in all activities of life.

I pledge allegiance to those who have gone before me, the ancestral lineage whose courage, sacrifice, and conviction still live in my bones. I honor the privileges given to me today because of the sweat from their pioneering efforts and the fortitude of their convictions. I give thanks for my responsibility in creating the same for future generations.

I pledge allegiance to a love that has no agenda. I no longer choose to give for what I might get, to manipulate in order to control, to abandon before I can be abandoned, to tolerate because there are seemingly no other options. I choose to love as a way of being. I am content in my choice whether outside circumstances respond or not. In being love, I create fulfillment above and beyond what the human condition can provide.

*I pledge allegiance to the sacredness of laughter, knowing that the greatest healing force that exists reverberates from the vibration of this holy and irreplaceable gift. I allow humor, joy, eruptions of laughter to make their home in my heart. I let my physical body respond to the sacred stimulus and biological wonder that laughter creates and vow to keep this attribute alive and thriving all the days of my life.**

In the comments section on Dr. Ault's YouTube channel, a viewer posted, "What a load of crap. Who can live like that? No one." I laughed out loud when I read that comment because I both disagree with and empathize with the commenter. The pledge describes such a high vision that it makes me wonder if I will ever be able to live that way. But that is precisely what a vision is supposed to do: take us beyond what we already know we can do, stretch us

* David Ault, "A New Pledge of Allegiance," http://davidault.com/a-new-pledge/. Used with permission.

into an idea that we have faith exists despite there being no evidence of it, yet. What use would a vision be if it only described things as they are right now? It's vital that each person uses their imagination to look beyond how things are currently to a greater yet-to-be. Think of it as a way of growing faith.

In 1912, Christian Larson wrote a pledge beginning with the words "Promise yourself." It is now known as the "Optimist Creed":

> *Promise yourself to be so strong that nothing can disturb your peace of mind. To talk health, happiness, and prosperity to every person you meet. To make all your friends feel that there is something worthwhile in them. To look at the sunny side of everything and make your optimism come true. To think only the best, to work only for the best, and to expect only the best. To be as enthusiastic about the success of others as you are about your own. To forget the mistakes of the past and press on to the greater achievements of the future. To wear a cheerful countenance at all times and give every living creature you meet a smile. To give so much time to the improvement of yourself that you have no time to criticize others. To be too large for worry, too noble for anger, too strong for fear, and too happy to permit the presence of trouble.**

Optimist International uses it as a creed of their organization. The original goes on for two more sentences:

> *To think well of yourself and to proclaim this fact to the world, not in loud words but great deeds. To live in faith that the whole world is on your side so long as you are true to the best that is in you.*

---

* Christian D. Larson, *Your Forces and How to Use Them* (London: Global Grey, 2013).

That's a tall order indeed, and it may seem out of reach for many people. However, if that were the price of admission for a life of freedom and happiness, would I be willing to pay it? What use would a pledge be if it merely acknowledged how things are right now? Is it helpful to promise to ourselves that we will not try to stretch and that we will not meddle with the way things are, or that we will settle for a baseline of average living as a way of coping with this life? Imagine the "Optimist Creed" without the visionary elements that make it so great:

> *I promise not to disturb myself, to be friendly only to those who deserve it, to be happy when things are going well, to trust those who earn it, to hold on to the past until amends are made, to point out accurately where others can improve themselves.*

That kind of low use of my imagination doesn't lead to freedom and happiness. I have to stretch by looking—beyond what is already possible and beyond what I already know—to something larger. Wouldn't it be wonderful if we had an annual tradition of writing our promises to ourselves or our personal creeds, and if we would renew them annually as a way of refreshing our commitment to growing? I believe that doing so is how we earn faith.

Group Mind

Among the many influences exercising control over our lives, making us feel like we are not free to experience goodness, is group mind—a theoretical psychic unity or the set of attitudes and beliefs that give a group its identity. This need not be a bad thing, and it wouldn't be if those shared beliefs were predominantly like Dr. David Ault's "New Pledge of Allegiance" or Christian Larson's "Optimist Creed." The trouble is that the preponderance of belief in popular thinking tends less toward being affirmative in tone and dwells more on urgency, disaster, and imminent danger. By a very early age, American teenagers who go to the movies, watch TV, and play video games will have witnessed an extraordinary number of brutal murders. They have possibly participated in the murders themselves while playing video games. The prevalence of violence in the media they consume may have desensitized them to aggression and disharmony. It's not that goodness is absent in our communities; it's that our focus is disoriented currently by the disproportionate amount of ugliness paraded about as ordinary entertainment.

What, in your opinion, is the general character of your community's group mind? Or of your family's? Most importantly, how has that general character become normal to your way of thinking? For example, my family's mind-set about the world contained simultaneously splendid and disturbing ideas. On one hand, I learned from my family that it is important to share because it shows that you care; it is important to be kind, because it shows you are loving; and it is important to be truthful and honest, because it shows that you are a good person. Much of that, fortunately, has taken root in me, and it would be a good thing for me to refresh my commitment to those group-mind ideas from my family regularly. On the other hand, I also learned some unhelpful ideas from my family, ideas that took root in me and shaped the adult I grew up to be. For example, I learned it is important to worry because it shows that you are realistic. And I learned it is important to hide your feelings because it shows you are considerate, and it is important to know what others need without being told, because that is how you can tell you genuinely love them. I absorbed some of both the helpful and the unhelpful ideas. I trusted my adult role models to impart accurate information about the way life works. Because I trusted them, I didn't question whether what was normal in my family would be normal or accurate in the rest of the world.

Group mind ideas can steal our experience of goodness when we don't scrutinize them. When we pledge allegiance to ways of behaving, without knowing why we are doing so, we are living according to someone else's faith. When we accept limitations, such as those associated with gender, color, or age, for example, because it is "normal" to do so, or when we fear those who don't fit in with the groupthink, and we don't know what the source of our fear is, we are not earning our faith. Voltaire wrote that every person is the creature of the age in which they live, and he was of the opinion that very few among us can raise ourselves above the ideas of our time. This is an accurate statement, but this situation doesn't have to be permanent. Equipped with our ordinary goodness, our natural-born instinct to love, our willingness to question and investigate our thinking, and regular rededications to visionary ideas that lift us up out of the ordinary, we can raise ourselves above the ideas of our time. We can escape from our conditioning. We can—and must—use our infinite, creative imaginations to look up from where we are and beyond current circumstances to a greater way of expressing our natural goodness. We can—and should—expect this kind of vision to pull us forward into freedom and happiness. We earn our faith by being willing to risk this type of inner work when there is little support from the group mind.

To earn my faith, I have to ask myself these questions: Do I have the courage to rise above the ideas of my time? Can I survive what people will think of me if I am more authentically myself? Am I willing to step outside of "the way it is" and live according to the true call of my soul? Will I choose my life, or will I live according to the script handed to me by the group mind?

Practice

Looking Deep Within

Faith, intimacy, and deepness take time. You can practice going deep with your contemplation by selecting a passage from an inspiring book, such as Christian Larson's *The Pathway of Roses*—for example, this passage from Newt List's gender-neutral edition*:

> *To give the world emancipation is the ruling desire of all minds that are spiritually awakened, and these minds should remember that overcoming evil with good is the only way. Forget the wrong that may appear in the outer world of things, and give all your thought to the great good that is inherent in all things. You thereby place in action the greatest emancipating power the human race will ever know.*

Use this, or the passage of your choice, every morning for one whole week to develop a close relationship with the text. Consider using it in one or all of the following ways:

- Read it first thing in the morning, followed by a few moments of silence.
- First thing in the morning, get a journal and pen and copy the text into it. Writing by hand has the effect of slowing down the mind. The slower pace allows you to take in the meaning of the text you have chosen to use.
- First thing in the morning, read the text. Pay attention to any sentences that have particular resonance for you. By resonance, I mean that the sentence seems relevant to your life, or

* Christian Larson, *The Pathway of Roses: Updated and Gender-Neutral* (Chicago: Newt List, 2015).

you experience an emotional response to reading it. Select one such sentence to commit to memory.

- For a more contemporary approach, first thing in the morning retype the text into your social media status followed by a request for comments.
- First thing, rewrite it in the first person. "The ruling desire of my mind is to give freedom to the world. The only way for me to go is with good. I think about the great good that is inherent in all things. I am using the greatest emancipating power in the world."
- Rewrite the phrase in your own words.

Faith as Something Given

How You Can Help Develop Other People's Faith with Your Ordinary Kindness

My grandmother bought a piano for me when I was a teen. The gift itself was a lovely gesture, but considering my family's financial circumstances, it was a stretch of epic size. We were poor, and people in our neighborhood typically did not have access to the luxury of a piano. To buy a piano was an extravagance that I never thought would be possible for our family. We had other more pressing needs. So when the opportunity to take piano lessons at school presented itself, I had enrolled without telling my parents and regardless of the fact that I had no piano at home to practice on. From the start, I showed some musical talent, and my teachers encouraged me to keep studying. I took the music lessons at school, but without a piano, I could not practice between lessons. My teacher didn't know I had no piano, and no one at home knew I was learning to play. I guess my family thought I had an active imagination when they saw me playing the kitchen table as if it were a keyboard. I didn't want to burden them with the need for a piano. My youthful plan of secrecy had a major flaw, though. I did not consider that my parents would eventually receive a bill and have to pay for the lessons. Unbeknownst to me, the teacher contacted my parents, and the whole thing came out. No one told me that my parents, in collaboration with the teacher, then made arrangements for me to continue to have lessons without charge. I didn't know I showed promise. I didn't know that my grandmother insisted that my family trust a talent they had no evidence existed other than the testimony of a teacher who hadn't been paid for six months.

One day I came home, and there was a piano in the living room. The family was gathered around it, waiting for me. Although my grandmother had furnished the lion's share of the cost from her savings, others had contributed and had gone without something so that they could help with the purchase my grandmother made. They wanted me to have an experience that none of them had had. I'll not easily forget their glowing faces when I walked into the living room after school, and neither will I forget the surge of appreciation I felt when I realized what they had done. My mother said, "Well, can you play anything at all?"

When I sat down at the new piano to play, no one knew what to expect. They had no idea that I had progressed as far as I had and had learned so much without an instrument to practice on. Another scene I won't forget is the look on their faces when I flawlessly completed a piece I had been learning. I could see that my music had made every one of their sacrifices worthwhile. In the scheme of things, a piano and music lessons are small, possibly insignificant. But to me they were everything. I was given something so much more than a musical instrument that day. I was given faith in loving-kindness. And I gave my family members something too. They received the gift of knowing that their contribution, no matter the smallness of it, had given me greater access to a world of music. And as significant as the gift was to me, the really meaningful contribution they had made to me came even before the piano arrived. It came in small gestures of affection, in moments of accepting my fanciful table playing, in words of affirmation, in generosity of spirit. Despite what we didn't have, and despite the hardships of coping with a disabled brother, we were giving each other the gift of faith in human kindness.

Marian Wright Edelman, the first African-American woman to be admitted to the Mississippi bar and the founder of the Children's Defense Fund (a voice for underprivileged, minority, and disabled children), said that we must not, when we are thinking about how to make a difference in our world, ignore the small daily contributions we make, which over time add up to a big contribution we often cannot predict.

My grandmother paid attention to everything that we did. She considered everything about us to be significant and worth supporting. She helped me understand that everything of value in my life existed because of the contributions, and even sacrifices, of someone else. In turn, my actions will someday make a contribution to someone else. Someone is always listening to what you or I have to say and then integrating our example into their lives. Someone is watching what we do and then choosing what they are going to do. We affect each other; we can't help it. Most of us want to leave the world better than we found it. We want to make a difference and leave a positive impression. We want to contribute something worthwhile and valuable. Perhaps we don't realize that we are already doing so, but every time we choose love over fear or forgiveness instead of resentment, we create ripples of goodness that, in my opinion, affect everyone on the planet.

Faith as Something Shared

How Faith Doesn't Necessarily Mean That Everything Works Out in the End

One of my coworkers in the nonprofit organization where I work epitomized the consciousness of selfless service. By consciousness, I mean everything that makes a person what they are, their overall theme. Everything that made my colleague who she was had to do with sharing. She shared her time, her efforts, her attention, and her words of encouragement wherever there was an opening for them. She seemed to be able to put other people first consistently, and loved doing it. One day she went into the hospital for a routine medical procedure on a facial nerve that was troubling her. During the procedure, she had a stroke and was not expected to survive. She had prepared health-care directives indicating that she did not wish to have any interference in her process or any further medical procedures. When I went to visit her, I found her room covered with flowers and cards. One of the nurses asked me quietly, "Is this person a celebrity?"

"Yes," I replied, "to me and to many others, she most certainly is."

She *was* a celebrity, not in the sense of a movie star, but as a well-loved grandmother figure to many more than her family members. She was a particular kind of celebrity, a role model for ordinary goodness. She did not seek acclaim, recognition, or status. I had a conversation with her children and explained that their mother had touched the lives of literally thousands of people through her work at our organization. One of them said, "I'm starting to see that she has been the mother to more people than to our immediate family."

She was tireless, loyal, and supporting. When someone needed to be comforted, Marilyn was there to do it. When it was time for me to be ordained as a minister, I had to select someone to present me in the ceremony, and I chose Marilyn. Someone asked me why I chose her when I could have chosen any number of officials of high standing. I explained that I chose her because she never asked me for a thing. She never asked for any recognition or position of prominence in our community. She served without needing attention. She was, to me, the kind of person who could retain humility and in so doing reduce rivalry around her. She was confident in her service and had no desire to possess or mimic the talents or skills of others. She shared who she was with effortlessness and reliability. To me, she was of very high standing.

After Marilyn had her stroke, I experienced some disorientation. My sadness affected my attention, and not surprisingly, I started misplacing and forgetting things. One day I left my wallet in the local supermarket. It was stuffed with $100 bills I had received from a friend paying back in cash a loan I had made to him. I didn't expect to find the wallet, let alone reclaim the money. Nevertheless, I drove back to the supermarket and checked in at customer service, where the service manager smiled broadly back at me and said, "Ahh, we've been waiting for you." Someone had found the wallet and turned it in with everything intact. The finder did not want to leave their name. I was touched, and my faith in humanity and my trust in ordinary goodness were renewed a little more that day, and it reminded me that I want to be like that. I want to be like Marilyn. I want to be like my grandmother. I want to be like honest strangers. I want to be like the coroner. I want to have faith in ordinary goodness.

Not knowing who the honest stranger was, and not having Marilyn around, presented me with an opportunity to carry their examples of sharing forward and to not let their gestures end with me. I attribute my habit of sharing to them and people like them whose sharing has inspired me to do the same.

Practice

Paying It Forward

A good habit to foster is the practice of paying it forward, which is the practice of doing something good for another person in response to something done for you. Instead of repaying the person, do something nice for someone else. One of the beneficial aspects of this practice is that it focuses on a spirit of selflessness, turning away from the expectation of reciprocation or recognition. There are, nevertheless, personal benefits that come from the practice of paying it forward, in that it helps diffuse the sense of the world being hostile and frightening. It can help an ordinary person, using ordinary goodness, contribute to the way others see our world by creating real relief and gaining a sense of meaning and connection. I call this sharing faith. For this exercise, begin to pay attention to the people around you. Notice where opportunities exist for helping. Offer to help carry groceries for a fellow shopper, offer to pick up groceries for a neighbor when you're planning to go shopping, open the door for someone who is carrying things, let someone go ahead of you in line.

For more information about paying it forward, visit www.payitforwardfoundation.org, a nonprofit organization that promotes acts of kindness among strangers to foster a more caring society.

Faith as Intuition

How Faith Doesn't Necessarily Make Common Sense

Hans Selye, the Austrian-Canadian endocrinologist, who is considered by some to be the first scientist to demonstrate the existence and effects of biological stress, said, "The fairest thing we can experience is the mysterious. It is the fundamental emotion which stands at the cradle of true science. He who knows it not, and can no longer wonder, no longer feel amazement, is as good as dead. We all had this priceless talent when we were young. But as time goes by, many of us lose it. The true scientist never loses the faculty of amazement. It is the essence of his being."* When I was a child, it was easier for me to feel amazement. I didn't need logical explanations for life to make sense like I do today. Even when I invented games to play, I didn't need the rules to make sense. If I managed to convince an adult or a friend to play with me, I would take care to explain my rules carefully. Inevitably one of

* *Newsweek*, March 31, 1958; http://todayinsci.com/S/Selye_Hans/SelyeHans-Quotations.htm.

my explanations would be met with the question "Why?" It was exasperating to me because I didn't know why. I only knew that when I created the rules, they seemed necessary. So I would answer, "Just because!," which was equally exasperating to my playmates. It turns out that I was more like my grandmother than I cared to admit. Apparently, I did have the capacity to trust without clear evidence. I relied on "Just because" to explain a lot of things I knew but didn't know how I knew them. I used it to explain things I didn't understand but was certain of. For example, if I was asked, "Why do you like your brother?," my idea of an entirely complete and proper answer would be "Just because." My mother used a similar technique when I asked her why she forbade me to do something. She probably inherited it from my grandmother, like I did. She would answer, "Just because," or the more definitive version, "Because I said so!"

I have to be careful not to let my childhood sense of amazement slip away completely. As an adult, I tend to look for a logical explanation for my decisions so that they can make sense. I want people to feel confident that I'm a reasonable person, thinking through things correctly, when in reality inside I can be wading through a messy trail of intuitive nudges that make little sense. Now and then, I might be prompted to do, say, or think something, but because it seems out of step with conventional wisdom, I might suppress my ideas and go with the popular choice instead. People tell me they too hide their intuitive process for fear of a wrinkled-up-nose response of "Why would you do that?" to which they have no response. The upside of making commonsense decisions is that people around me feel more confident that I have valid reasons for making them. But the downside is that my sensitivity to my felt experience of knowing begins to decrease as I start to downplay its role in my thinking.

Even though I may try to distance myself from the mysterious process I call intuition, I have never quite managed to do so. After all, who hasn't had an idea in the middle of the night to make a course correction in life? It might be an illogical choice that makes everyone say, "You're crazy," with solid reasons to back up their reaction, and when you take a moment to think about it, their objection to your idea may be reasonable. Yet you can't shake the feeling of rightness about making the change, and you don't know the answer to the question "Why?" other than to say sheepishly, "Just because."

Intuition is like that: difficult to measure and test. We feel things, and we know things in ways that we cannot define or explain. Those inner promptings are not always precise or reliable, but they are there in us just the same. To me, intuition is our ability to know without the process of reasoning. It can provide a rich source of great ideas for our lives that get us excited to go ahead and do great things that no amount of careful planning and analysis can achieve. Developing sensitivity to that intuitive faculty takes resilience because there is doubt about its reliability, and rightly so—it is difficult to sort through the difference between intuition, fantasy, cultural messages, and everything else floating around inside our minds. Nevertheless, even with all these known issues, when we disconnect from our intuition we deprive ourselves of one of the greatest and most beautiful navigation-assistance systems we have. We ought not to lose contact with it. Instead, we might adopt an adventurer's attitude and listen to what we are prompted to do from within. The more people are aware of and in touch with their ordinary goodness, the more they can depend on their intuition. It will not prompt them to do something dangerous to themselves or to others. If you and I are prompted from within to do something dangerous, vicious, or mean-spirited, that isn't intuition, and it ought not to be followed. That's not to say intuition will never nudge you out onto the skinny branch of faith, or never suggest you take the step you are nervous to take—it probably will. But it doesn't, in my opinion, recommend reckless, violent, and irresponsible actions. Ordinary goodness is not about that, it's about life and trust and creativity. Sometimes intuition suggests a grand idea about your life or even a weird idea, and you may have a healthy dose of appropriate second-guessing to go through. You may also encounter opposition from friends and family and a feeling that no one understands you.

The famous chemist and inventor of Vaseline, Sir Robert Augustus Chesebrough, could not get anyone to take his new product seriously. He had to burn himself and apply the salve to his own wounds in front of audiences to demonstrate what Vaseline was capable of. I don't advocate hurting yourself to convince people around you, but the story does remind me that sometimes you have to be your own authority and take action on your good ideas, even if no one understands why you are doing so, and especially if you feel strongly that your intuition is prompting you to act. When respected experts and trusted friends tell us something is not a good idea, we may be challenged to decide between listening to them or to the prompts from our intuition that lead us toward our good. Understanding what our good is can be tricky too. Aristotle used the word *good* to mean "that at which all things aim."* But what is good for me may not be good for you. I can also have an idea of what is right for me, which may not actually be healthy. Take, for example, passion for success, or obsession with love, or dependence on substances. Again, it may be difficult to sort out which inner urges to follow. What is a prompt from intuition and what is not? We can practice developing sensitivity to intuition to more easily identify it. But even if we do, it won't always make the

---

* Aristotle, *Nicomachean Ethics*, Book I, Internet Classics Archive, http://classics.mit.edu/Aristotle/nicomachaen.1.i.html.

kind of logical sense that satisfies our intellect, possibly because it communicates in feelings and images, and requires interpretation, flexibility, and not taking it too seriously.

Practice
Noticing

To practice being more tuned in to intuition, you'll need an open mind and the willingness to spend some time pursuing it with mindfulness and sensitivity. Other than that, the most important aspect of your assignment is to pay attention to what is going on in and around you, beyond the chatter of your mind. For many people, the content of their thoughts occupies all their attention, crowding out the possibility of noticing anything else. Without adding judgment about the content of your thoughts, try to pay attention to life in this way: imagine you're watching a movie you've seen many times before, so many times that you can let your attention stray from the central action on the screen and pay attention to peripheral activities and objects. Ask yourself, what else is there in the scene that I didn't notice before? A movie enthusiast might watch movies in this way and take pleasure in finding continuity errors or out-of-place props and extras out of character, all for fun. Approach your exercise with as much fun as you can muster, and look for what's going on. Try to notice what you usually don't see.

Once you get the hang of it, you can add another level of depth to your practice by actively looking for sequences, patterns, and coincidences. And if you are feeling particularly playful, experiment with interpreting what they mean. If you see three red cars in a row, ask yourself, "What could that mean?" Be open to whatever you come up with. Try not to edit your process. You are developing the skill of being a mindful observer of your inner and outer life, and this will develop your sensitivity to your intuition.

PART FIVE

Finding Faith

Whenever we turn to God, there is a light that shines and burns in us, guiding us as to what we should do and what we should not do, and giving us many other kinds of good instruction, of which we had no knowledge or understanding in the past.*

—*Meister Eckhart*

---

* Meister Eckhart, *Selected Writings* (New York: Penguin Books, 1994), 216–17.

Co-Existence

The Place Where Faiths Intersect

The Indonesian island of Bali is about 90 percent Hindu and 10 percent Muslim in a country that is 90 percent Muslim. On a recent pilgrimage to Bali with a group of American travelers, I asked our young Hindu driver what it was like to live as a minority in the country, and how he got along with the majority of Muslims from the other islands. He answered saying that they mostly get along with each other; where they collide is not in person-to-person contacts but in those places where their cultural practices get in each other's way. I asked for an example. He explained that Muslims surrender to prayer five times a day, and the first call to prayer is before the sun rises. The beautiful call comes from the minaret of the mosque, broadcast over loudspeakers in poetic language. The problem is that approximately at that same time, directly before sunrise, Hindus are preparing to embrace the holy silence of their most sacred time of day for meditation. The Balinese Hindus whom I know are expert at compromise and accommodation. Perhaps this is because they are a minority and have had to learn that skill, or because both they and their Muslim compatriots see the advantage of peaceful coexistence and are putting peace before preferences. Somehow, the islanders make it work.

I asked my Hindu driver if he had any Muslim friends. He said yes. I asked what differences he saw between Muslims and Hindus. He said that in his younger generation, there are fewer and fewer noticeable differences. I asked if the two groups were a good or bad influence on each other. He found the question delightful and said maybe good, maybe bad, because young Hindus are seeing a much simpler prayer practice in their Muslim friends' daily spiritual obligations than what is expected of Hindus. And young Muslims are seeing what they perceive as more freedom among their Hindu friends in social matters.

Whether the views of these young people are accurate or whether their elders would approve, I don't know. I do suspect that what my young friend was describing to me is exactly what happens when we get to know each other, live together, and talk together. It can be eye-opening to ask about and learn about other people's beliefs and practices. What we discover can at first seem strange until we learn from them that our ways are strange to them too. For example, take Easter as it is practiced today in the United States. Try to explain that to a Balinese Muslim or Hindu millennial. I did try, and it is not easy to make logical sense out of it. You have to deal with the bunnies, eggs, hats, chocolates, and all the paraphernalia they see in movies, news, and social networks. You have to explain all of that, even before you can get to the important part about the death, resurrection, ascension, and transfiguration of the central figure of Christianity. The same goes for Christmas as it is today. Try explaining Christmas to a Thai or to any millennial and make sense out of it. You would have to explain gift-giving, evergreen trees chopped down and brought indoors, various characters, from Saint Nicholas to Santa Claus, carols, candlelight vigils, midnight masses, and yule logs, all without any scriptural references to support you. It can be exasperating.

When it comes to faith and belief, logic often has to take a backseat. I'm okay with that, as long as I can extend the courtesy to others and acknowledge that one way of believing can be as out-there as any other. I read a posting on the Internet that, I'm guessing, was meant to be funny. I took it with a pinch of salt, as a humorous reminder that ways of believing are diverse and can be strange and curious to me, in the same way mine are to others. The posting read something like: *Homosexuality is abnormal. It says so in a book where snakes talk, people come back from the dead, live for hundreds of years, own slaves, walk on water, and a virgin has a baby.*

I see the value in allowing others to have and enjoy their way of believing. I don't care to change or convert them to something else. As I explore faith traditions of the world, each has its share of colorful and interesting ways of believing. Christianity, Hinduism, Judaism, Islam, Buddhism, paganism, New Thought—each has some form of supernatural phenomena, paranormal events, various dimensions of being, and some freedom of choice or self-awareness. However, I haven't yet found anything, in any faith's description, that helps me understand the point of a supreme being that creates beings with the potential to fail and then tests them. I don't get that. It seems beneath what a supreme intelligence ought to produce. But as a metaphor, I get it, because sometimes life sure does feel like a test: Will I call upon my ordinary goodness and choose a compassionate life of coexistence, or will I go the other way?

Mystery

How Different Practices Reveal the Same Mystery

I've done a good deal of looking around at various religions for a place to land and dig in. It seems to me that many spiritual traditions have at least two parts that are connected to each other. One part deals with the practices of the tradition, and the other part deals with the results of the practices (in other words, the potential of what happens if one engages in the practices of the tradition). Each faith has its own guidelines for how to live, how to pray and meditate, and how to think. Buddhism's practical Eightfold Path, for example, guides adherents through the tricky business of being in this world and trying to attain self-awareness. Islam's Five Pillars is another example, one that lays out the essentials of charity, pilgrimage, daily prayer, fasting, and declaring the faith. Faith traditions generally, and each in its own way, offer practical guidance for everyday life, touching on prayer, meditation, selfless service, study, charity, and gratitude. Through the prescribed practices, adherents connect with and exercise their ordinary goodness, and are led to an encounter with something beautiful.

Typically, part two of spiritual systems deals with this encounter. I call it the mystery. And, it seems, one can't meet the mystery without engaging in the practice.

I am inclined to take shortcuts. I often think I don't need to read the entire user manual when I get a new device or tool. I don't like to delay enjoyment by following all the steps in a do-it-yourself project. In my exploration of religions, I did the same. I wanted to bypass the practices and drop into the mystical awareness that each offered. What I discovered, however, is that the doorway to the mystery is closed and can be opened only by those who practice. It reminded me of my days as a music teacher. I had students who wanted to play a concerto, but who wouldn't practice playing scales to develop their technique. As a result, their music was always superficial, and the blissful experience of masterfully performing was out of their reach and forever would remain that way, so long as they had no practice.

As a young man, I became fascinated with yoga. Because I was competitive, I focused intently on learning all the poses so that I could do them better and hold them longer than anyone else in the class. I aimed to learn all the names of the poses in Sanskrit and what the names meant. Fortunately, I was consistent and practiced regularly, and this saved me from a superficial practice. The regular engagement allowed my yoga to deepen in me even though my focus was initially on winning the competition. The serenity of actually doing poses with care and attention leads a person away from competition and inevitably inward to contemplation. It worked like magic for me, and I found myself experiencing states of calm and connectedness that would not have been available to me had I not begun the journey of yoga. I discovered that learning to meditate was the same process. At first, sitting quietly was cumbersome, awkward, and even unenjoyable. But I stayed with it, patiently moving through my moments of rebellion and disappointment with my busy mind. Eventually, the consistency of my practice opened up the doorway to an experience of profound peace.

The experiences I had in meditation and yoga led me to appreciate what mystics of some faiths have touched upon. I began to understand how their practices might lead them to a state of mind that is available only to those who practice, whether they be Muslim, Jew, Buddhist, or something else. I suspect that there is a cumulative effect of practicing one's faith, whatever it may be, that leads to an awareness of what some call the "ultimate nature of existence." I call it "the mystery." It's a mystery because when we do experience it, it is difficult to describe it to people who have not experienced it. It seems that, regardless of the form of practice, there is a point where the differences between religions fall away—and those who practice begin to use similar language to describe their experiences. It is as if the various practices lift a veil and reveal a shared landscape.

When life is challenging, the idea of encountering this mystery is simply not interesting to some. Other things may seem to be rightly more important. Who cares about ultimate reality if they have been laid off unexpectedly and have a family to feed and a mortgage to pay, or when a relationship changes in what seems an annoying way, or a loved one dies? At times like these, the practices of our faith are supposed to come to our assistance. They are supposed to teach us what to do when we are sad, where to go when we are lonely, how to work with our minds when they are frantic, and how to cope with life. That is the function of spiritual practices. Through them, even though our attention may be fragmented at first, and no matter the particular form we have chosen for our faith, we gradually approach the doorway that opens to what we cannot know without practice.

It matters more that the practice is conducted faithfully, and less what the particular practice is. What I mean is that when something is practiced regularly, over time, the act of practicing surpasses the actual steps. As with learning to play a musical instrument, eventually the repetitive focus on scales yields to an experience of music. That experience comes whether you choose to play the flute or the piano. On my journey of spiritual exploration, I began to notice the different ways people practice, and when I stopped focusing on the differences, I began to see that those who faithfully practice tend to travel in the same direction: ordinary goodness.

My exploration of spiritual life began by way of the New Age movement and its fascinating mix of practices. The blend was so broad, though, that it was a challenge for me to achieve lasting deepness. I was applying too many methods at once without giving any one of them regular, focused attention. I might have taken my grandmother's warning not to become a jack-of-all-trades, but master of none. But I did not heed her words. I was like a hummingbird, darting around in fascination from practice to practice, burning it all up and still hungry. I didn't stay with any single practice long enough to get to the depth of understanding I wanted. I know some people who have effectively created a daily personal practice through borrowing from different traditions. The difference between them and me is that once they built their particular practice, they practiced it devoutly! I continued to look around and try on more and more. The difference between shallowness and deepness, I discovered, is between leaning faithfully into something versus having a casual and shallow relationship with it. I began to appreciate the difference between being a tourist and being a resident.

Thirteen years ago, I started visiting Bali and have taken groups back there almost annually, sometimes more than once a year, on pilgrimages to learn about the unique form of Balinese Hinduism and to visit the sacred sites. Over the years, friendships have developed. Familiarity has deepened. Nuances became apparent about the people and culture. At first, I could not detect the little details, and only after I had traveled to Bali many, many times did I begin to notice them. I also travel with groups on spiritual pilgrimages to other destinations, but because I visit those destinations less frequently, my depth of understanding of the culture remains more on the surface.

When I was a young man, I was anxious to discover the right and best spiritual practice, and I let my eagerness hurry me through matters that require more thoughtfulness. I'm calmer now and no longer feel the need to dip into every ocean. I have seen that all who practice eventually encounter the mystery. Christians meet it, Muslims encounter it, pagans discover it, and so on. I believe there is no such thing as a right faith, but there is such a thing as a right effort or a good attitude that leads to deepness. Depth grows through consistency and steadiness. I have seen that faithfulness to ordinary goodness in the form of daily kindness and compassion is itself a practice that leads to an experience of the mystery, with or without religion.

Understanding Mystics

Mystics are women and men who, because of their practice, reach a deep understanding of the nature of being. However, they don't necessarily become fanatical about the particular practices that open their understanding. Instead, they see their practice as one among many pathways to understanding. Mystics are not always understood in their time and culture, especially if their culture has become obsessed with the rules and form of a particular practice. I imagine a mystic emerging in a culture that is stuck in a tradition saying, "There is more to existence than these rules." That might be problematic if the rules have been helpful in bringing order to the chaos of cultural life. I can imagine the response of the leaders and people being "What do you mean? These rules are everything, and we have to follow them." In my imagined scenario, the mystic would say, "No, the rules are not divine; they are merely a pathway to travel on. Practice them, but don't let them become your gods." Margaret Smith describes mysticism as "the most vital element in all true religions, rising in revolt against cold formality and religious torpor."* It is easy to get stuck on a formal method, especially if it works. There is a difference between becoming fanatically fixed on a method and practicing it diligently. I have to watch that I don't cross the line and become fanatical because I have a tendency to be superstitious. For example, if I have good results with a particular spiritual practice, I'm likely to latch onto it; I become attached to it and am inclined to repeat it. When I do that, I'm missing the point. The way of the mystery is not confined to one particular path. Rumi, probably the best-known Muslim mystic in the Western world, and Christianity's Teresa of Ávila, Catherine of Siena, and Hildegard of Bingen—as well as the mystics of Judaism, Hinduism, and other faiths—are people who, through their different traditions, brought new insight into our world. They saw into the nature of being with the understanding that is only available, it seems, to those who regularly engage in their practice. Nevertheless, ordinary people like you and me can aspire to be our own kind of mystic by following their example. We can do so by selecting a spiritual practice and committing to it without becoming fanatical about it.

We can pick up clues about the mystical experience from elements mystics share in common, no matter that they come from different faiths. What follows are three elements I have noted. I think of them as items on a brochure describing what I can expect to gain if I train in a particular course of study.

---

* Margaret Smith, "The Nature and Meaning of Mysticism," in *Understanding Mysticism*, Richard Woods, ed. (London: Athlone Press, 1980), 20.

Embrace Paradox

The first item for consideration is that mystics embrace paradox. Their practice makes them intensely aware of life's paradoxes. They notice that although everything appears to be part of one unity, life contains many opposites. Everything is united, yet life is made up of endless polarities, such as good and bad, hot and cold, and so on. Mystics sense that things are not immediately what they appear to be and that focusing on the pairs of opposites distracts them from the experience of unity: they understand that reality is larger than the polar opposites that make it up. This inevitably causes them to loosen up and abandon narrow views of right/wrong, good/bad. They adopt an attitude of awe and wonder. I might put these words into the mouths of mystics: "Ordinary goodness is the norm—yet, simultaneously, humanity's free will is capable of producing suffering." Mystics, as Rumi did through his poetry, advise us to practice seeing beyond what can be seen with the physical eye. Close both eyes, he advised, to see with the other eye, and thereby peacefully embrace and see beyond the paradoxes of life.

Personal Relationship

The second quality among mystics is that they have a personal, intimate relationship with their concept of Divinity. Intimacy, as we learned earlier, takes time to nurture. A close relationship with Divinity, like an intimate relationship with a person, takes time and requires steadiness and consistency. You have to share yourself and show yourself. You have to be consistent and present. You have to be transparent and caring to create the environment for intimacy to grow. It is the same with developing a relationship with your concept of Divinity, or with life, or reality, if you prefer.

Live in the World

The third quality among mystics, especially the kind of modern mystic that you and I might aspire to become, is that they continue to have ordinary worldly experiences. Although they see the bigger picture, although they embrace paradox, and although they have a close, personal relationship with Divinity, they nevertheless continue to live in this world. In other words, they probably have bills to pay, families to raise, jobs to deal with, and problems to solve. Sometimes they get sick, and sometimes their children don't turn out the way they hoped. Sometimes they make terrible mistakes, and sometimes they get crucified, and sometimes their friends let them down. The difference is that they are strengthened, not so much because they have excellent coping mechanisms in place, but because they encountered the mystery. So now, living in the ordinary world with all its complexity and sadness seems to be a beautiful thing to them, because everything in it speaks to them about the unity of all life.

Rather than withdraw from life, mystics lean into it and bring goodness into being as a result of their inner realization.

Practice
Being a Mystic Yourself

How can we tap into our mysticism? Here are my suggestions:

Practice Daily

If you have a faith tradition, choose a practice from it to focus on, and give yourself a chance to develop a deep relationship with it. Take enough time for whatever practice you choose to use to become a daily routine. This way, you can move past the outward mechanics of becoming familiar with the practice and move beyond it into something more. If you do not have a faith tradition of your own, consider using one of the methods described in Sage Bennet's *Wisdom Walk: Nine Practices for Creating Peace and Balance from the World's Spiritual Traditions.*

Practice thinking thoughts of goodwill toward other people

Start a routine of thinking kindly about people. You can use whatever form of prayer you are accustomed to, or simply call the people to mind and imagine their well-being.

Practice being extraordinarily kind

Developing kindness takes subtlety and sensitivity. Kindness is not the same as being nice. You can be nice and still not care about the other person. You have to be sincere to be kind—and through sincerity you will start to see and feel what the mystics are talking about when they say all life is one.

Practice being present

Take time to be alone, to be silent. The most pleasant place for this exercise is outside in nature, if possible. If being outside is not feasible for your experience, select a place where you can be undisturbed. You only need five to fifteen minutes of alone time daily to begin a practice of enjoying being in the present moment. During your time alone, try to notice your environment, whether you are inside or outside.

Polarities

How Resolving Polarities of Good and Bad Is Not a Requirement for Ordinary Goodness

A friend was raising funds for a 545-mile bicycle ride from San Francisco to Los Angeles to benefit organizations serving people affected by HIV/AIDS. The AIDS/Lifecycle campaign at the time had the slogan "To Fight HIV." My friend approached a young woman for a donation, but she would not contribute to the fight against HIV. When she read the slogan on his smartphone app designed to receive on-the-spot donations, she said she opposed fighting anything. I understand her position. I prefer another slogan of this charity, "To End HIV," because it points to the same result without the language of combat. When I receive emails from the political party of my choice, they are frequently peppered with combative language to incite a state of urgency. The emails warn me about the imminent dangers of succumbing to the plans of the other political side and tell me of the importance of arming up through contributions for a battle against this or that. I feel disinclined to participate even when I believe in the cause being addressed. "For crying out loud, is there not a more beautiful way to express this?" I want to ask the campaigners. I want to reframe their language, as I once did with reference to a strongly worded statement that has been wrongly attributed to Meryl Streep, but is actually from Portuguese life coach José Micard Teixeira. The original reads:

> *I no longer have patience for certain things, not because I've become arrogant, but simply because I reached a point in my life where I do not want to waste more time with what displeases me or hurts me. I have no patience for cynicism, excessive criticism, and demands of any nature. I lost the will to please those who do not like me, to love those who do not love me and to smile at those who do not want to smile at me.*
>
> *I no longer spend a single minute on those who lie or want to manipulate. I decided not to coexist anymore with pretense, hypocrisy, dishonesty, and cheap praise. I do not tolerate selective erudition nor academic arrogance. I do not adjust either to popular gossiping. I hate conflict and comparisons. I believe in a world of opposites, and that's why I avoid people with rigid and inflexible personalities. In friendship, I dislike the lack of loyalty and betrayal. I do not get along with those who do not know how to give a compliment or a word of encouragement. Exaggerations bore me, and I have difficulty accepting those who do not like animals. And on top of everything I have no patience for anyone who does not deserve my patience.**

When I first read these paragraphs, I felt the way I imagined the young woman who didn't support fighting felt. I asked myself why the wrongly attributed quote was receiving such positive support in social media, and I did not want to support its furtherance.

* https://www.facebook.com/112342588846759/photos/a.131300700284281.34766.112342588846759/912291335518543/?type=3&theater.

I wondered why it hadn't been called out for being self-centered and arrogant or, at least, lacking compassion. I marveled at my own strong, snarky opinions about the piece and my inclination to go to battle with it.

I remembered, then, that giving expression to what I call natural goodness takes commitment and recommitment. It may need to be frequently renewed. So I sat with the quote and asked myself if there was, for me, a more beautiful way of saying the same thing. Looking at it line by line, I asked myself how I would restate each idea, and I wrote this:

I have reached a point in my life where I want to spend time on what brings joy and delight to me and those around me. I am drawn to those who have tolerance and patience and who exhibit concern for the well-being of others. I find great value in spending time with people who like me, who love me, and who want to share their smile with me.

I am drawn to those who love honesty and freedom. I notice that I like to collaborate with those who are transparent, genuine, and sincere. I love interacting with people who love to learn and who are sometimes uncertain about what they know. I am comfortable being out of step with popular trends, and I shy away from comparison as a form of motivation.

I value loyalty and forgiveness, and I cherish heartfelt encouragement both when giving and receiving it. I am fascinated by the diversity of human creativity, and I genuinely love those who show gentle loving-kindness to all beings. And on top of everything I am amazed that people accept and welcome me into their lives.

Does it lack the bite of the original? A little. Will the positive spin render the content uninteresting, like the content of those "good news" websites that struggle to gain a foothold in society? Maybe.

There is a prevailing idea in our culture that suggests we need conflict, urgency, and threats to remain engaged with life. I'm not suggesting that there are no such things as conflict, urgency, and threats. In reality, we have to address the difficulties of life rather than avoid them. We have to deal with slights from each other, perceived or real. Avoiding unpleasant situations or difficult subjects may seem preferable at times, but, realistically, if I refuse to have a conversation with people who disagree with my point of view or if I avoid people whose personalities disturb my peace of mind, I will have a difficult time being in this world. Joseph Campbell wrote: "So if you really want to help this world, what you will have to teach is how to live in it. And that, no one can do who has not himself learned how to live in it, in the joyful sorrow and sorrowful joy of the knowledge of this life as it is."*

Our lives are a balance of dynamic tension between the polarities of good and bad, pleasant and unpleasant, attractive and repellent. So when we read something like my rewrite above, if it is overly flattened into positivity, it may seem to be out of touch with reality. It may lack life's nuances and its ongoing struggle between opposing forces. At any moment, one of these polarities dominates over the other. To not acknowledge that life includes dark, hard, and challenging parts is to be unable to see life for what it is. At the same time, a description of reality as exclusively an endless battle between competing forces is also unsatisfying. Many search for something that they sense is simultaneously true: that there is a ground of all being, something permanently at peace, something that is enduring, upon which everything rests. In the Bhagavad Gita, Lord Krishna describes himself as the unchanging reality that gives rise to the

---

* Joseph Campbell, *Myths to Live By* (New York: Bantam Books, 1973).

endless forms of creation, and he warns Prince Arjuna not to be mistaken by thinking of the world of forms and opposites as all there is to his complete being. In a piece reminiscent of the Bhagavad Gita, American philosopher Ernest Holmes writes that we have such a presence within us. He describes it as a friend within:

> *This Friend within you is Infinite, and since it is Infinite, it is not limited by previous experiences which you may have had, by neither present conditions nor passing situations. It has no inherited tendencies of evil, lack, or limitation. It has never been caught in the mesh of circumstances. It is at all times radiant, free, and happy. It is your inner, absolute, and perfect Self. The Friend within you lives in a state of poise. It is above fear. It is beyond hurt. It is sufficient to Itself. There can be no greater unity than exists between you and this inner Friend. It spreads a table before you in the wilderness of human thought. Its cup of joy runs over. It laughs at disaster, triumphs over human failure, and mocks the grave. When this present experience shall be rolled up like a scroll, it will pass on to new and greater experiences. But today, this Friend is here. Trust It then, today, and you may trust it for all tomorrows yet to come. Possibly it will be difficult for you to believe that there is such a Friend, but it is there at the very center of your being, directing your thought and causing you to triumph over every defeat . . . for it is an unconquerable hero. The one who keeps silent watch within you, lifts your consciousness to the realization that you are forever protected, forever safe, forever perfect.*[*]

I don't know if there is a friend within, and I don't know if there is a changeless ground of all being. But I enjoy thinking

---

* Ernest Holmes, *Living the Science of Mind* (Camarillo, CA: DeVorss, 2012).

about what it might be like if indeed these things exist. I enjoy thinking that there is part of me that observes while I engage in life, something that remains untouched by the choices I make or how things turn out. I am aware of my intuitive nature, the power of contemplative practices to evoke the mystery of oneness and diversity, and sometimes when pressed, I'll call all of that the Divine.

Divinity

How Ordinary Goodness Caused Me to Redefine Divinity

My interest in ordinary goodness caused me to rethink what I had learned about God. I became more inclined to use the word *goodness* when talking about an overall and uniting power in life, almost as if it were a synonym. So I set about coming up with a definition for goodness to see where it, as a synonym for Divinity, would lead me. Defining God is not a simple task—in fact, it's impossible. If you begin with the really big ideas that one has to consider when thinking about the nature of the Divine—infinite, eternal, omnipresent, etc.—it becomes apparent, as the Tao Te Ching suggests, that the name we use to identify the Divine is probably not adequate or even accurate. I've found it helpful to set aside names and work with the pronoun "It" when exploring what the Divine means to me. The pronoun "It" helps me remember that I have put aside my childhood idea of a man in the sky, a white-bearded man, a benevolent dictator managing the affairs of the world. "It" frees me up from gender-specific terms and from the tendency to assign human qualities to the Divine. When I think of what "It" might be, I try to imagine something, like intelligence, that is the stuff out of which everything is made and also the potential for everything that ever will be made. I don't mind that I get all tangled up in trying to define it. I am on a quest to find a simple and easy way to describe it, and I keep discovering new ways to think about it and understand it, none of which are truly simple.

The words of Thaddeus Golas, in *The Lazy Man's Guide to Enlightenment*, may be the closest I've come to a simple definition of "It." He wrote, "The universe is made up of one kind of whatever-it-is, which cannot be defined. For our purpose, it isn't necessary to try to define it. All we need to do is assume that there is only one kind of whatever-it-is, and see if it leads to a reasonable explanation for the world as we know it."* That the universe is made up of one kind of whatever-it-is is a beautiful idea, but not simple. It births all sorts of questions, such as, why then is the world today in such poor shape? Cities are decaying, landfills are overflowing, and people are warring and starving. How do you explain all this in terms of everything being made up of one something?

I don't know the answers. I think of the phrase as more like a mission to accomplish than as a puzzle to solve. To me "The universe is made up of one kind of whatever-it-is" is a challenge to view the world as if it were all a product of one whatever-it-is and see if that leads to a deeper, more compassionate engagement with the world. In my experience, it does. It works particularly well for me to imagine that whatever-it-is is goodness. Specifically, it means to me that I try to look at each person I meet in a day as a being in

---

* Thaddeus Golas, *The Lazy Man's Guide to Enlightenment* (Encino, CA: The Seed Center, 1973).

which It dwells. It means treating everything in my environment as if it were treasured and beautiful because it is made from It.

In the course of a single day, I stray from my self-imposed mission of seeing It in everything dozens of times. I have to course-correct frequently to return to the view of oneness, and to me, this is exactly what living from ordinary goodness is all about. I find it worthwhile and rewarding to see how far into the day I can get before abandoning my commitment to goodness, and the effort and sincerity I put into this exercise seems to be of benefit to those around me also. I see now that the way we view Goodness—or Reality, or Divinity—changes based on where we are on our journey of awakening.

What Do You Believe?

Arthur Schopenhauer was of the opinion that hardly one in ten thousand will have the strength of mind to seriously and earnestly ask themselves, "Is that true?" I also think that very few people ask themselves seriously and earnestly, "What do I believe?" I heard a motivational speaker ask his audience, "If it were against the law to practice your particular faith, would there be enough evidence to convict you?" What evidence is there in your life that you believe what you believe? The real proof of what you believe is found in your behavior, in the way you handle yourself in the day-to-day activities of your life, how you are when you are at the top of the hill, and how you are when you are traveling through the bottom of a valley of despair. If anything, my hope is that *Ordinary Goodness* will have prompted you to think about what you believe, and to explore how it is that you came to believe the way you do, and then observe the impact your belief has on your choices.

Imagine that you've been invited to speak on national television. You have fifteen minutes to articulate what you believe. You don't have time to explain how it is you came to your belief, only enough time to say what you actually believe. What would you say? Getting clear on what you believe, and why you believe it, is an ongoing process. Even if you had a year to prepare for your television appearance, you would have to hold what you come up with lightly, so that it can evolve and change with you. Think of it as becoming clear on something you have always believed—so clear that you can confidently share it with others and, more importantly, clear to yourself so that you can make whatever adjustments are necessary so that your life mirrors what you say you believe.

I try to keep Neale Donald Walsch's words in mind: "There is no truth except the truth that exists within you. Everything else is what someone is telling you."* It is my hope that this exploration of ordinary goodness, ordinary kindness, ordinary compassion, and ordinary faith will do for you what it has done for me: help me get clearer on what I believe and what I stand for. I have found that if I keep in mind these four big concepts I have everything I need to live a life of meaning and value. I try to keep in mind that what I believe today is a function of where I am, the challenges and joys I'm experiencing, the consistency of my meditation practice, and so many other factors. I try to have the strength of mind to regularly question if what I believe is true. Below I share what I currently believe in the hope that you will be inspired to answer the question for yourself. I don't know what you're facing in your life or what caused you to read this book. Perhaps your life is working very well and you're looking for a way to celebrate that, or maybe you are looking for an answer to a question that troubles you or you are seeking relief from a challenge. Whatever it is that brought

---

* Neale Donald Walsch, *Home with God: In a Life That Never Ends* (New York: Atria Books, reprint edition, 2007), 14.

you this far, I am confident that your natural-born goodness is a power within you that is able to meet your need and carry you to the next meaningful step in your life. Moreover, the world is hungry for role models of ordinary people like you and me, living their lives from their belief in ordinary goodness as best we can, moment to moment.

Practice
What Do You Believe?

Thinking of the imagined television appearance above, take some time to consider what you believe as if you had accepted the invitation. Use the four central topics of this book to guide you, and form your answers by asking yourself, "What do I believe about goodness, kindness, compassion, and faith?" I have been thinking about these questions for a very long time, and my answers evolve as I observe and understand more and more about life. As of writing this, here is approximately what I believe.

What I Believe

I believe that Hell is a state of mind. I believe that Heaven is a state of mind. I believe that there is one "whatever-it-is" and I call it Spirit. I think of it as the One Source from which all creation originates. That's what I mean when I say Spirit is all there is. Everything comes from It and everything is contained within It. I encounter many terms used by different cultures and theologies to express this concept of Oneness. Some of them I like more than others. The ones I appreciate the most are those that each person discovers for himself or herself. Whether someone calls It the Thing Itself, Spirit, Life, Love, First Cause, Love-Intelligence, the Absolute, Universal Mind, the Changeless, the Universe,

Infinite Knowingness, the Supreme Being, the Divine Presence, or something else, I believe they are talking about the same thing, that which Emerson called the Oversoul, some Native Americans call the Great Spirit, and Lao-Tzu called the Tao. And I believe that despite my feeling of separateness, this oneness is irrevocable and eternal, and can never be lost, damaged, diminished, or destroyed throughout my life's journey. It is who I am.

I believe that right now and forever, I am a product of this oneness. I have heard this expressed as being a child of God, or being a channel for Spirit, or being an outlet for creation, or being a point of inspiration within the mind of the Creator. Whatever the correct phrase is, I believe that we inherit the nature of whatever process created us. And by that I mean that we are creative and that we are incredibly powerful, and that we are waking up to use our creative power for good more and more every day. And as we do so, we realize that the more we train our thought to dwell upon our true nature, the less we are victims of inherited ideas that serve neither us nor anyone else.

I believe there is a natural law of order that runs through the universe. I believe that we can see that law in action in our lives when we begin to notice the relationships between giving and receiving, sowing and reaping, and thinking and creating. And I believe that misunderstanding or ignoring these natural balances does not excuse me, or anyone, from the consequences of living out of harmony with them.

And, furthermore, I believe that this One whatever-it-is has no center, no circumference, and no limits, was never created, and cannot be uncreated. It never started and never ends, and so I call it infinite. And infinite to me means abundant and abundant to me means more than I can imagine. So I look at the numbers of physical forms that surround me, and they confirm it through the endless supply of pollen, sand on a beach, drops of rain. I look to the numbers of ideas that pour through us and result in miraculous inventions and marvelous works of art, and I realize I am part of that. This infinite bounty is the birthright of every being. And it occurs to me to share what I have learned so people everywhere can shake loose from the inherited repressive ideas hidden in them that tell them otherwise. I believe that there is something fundamentally right with the world and that every being can experience it or be supported in experiencing a more vibrant life. I believe kindness is the most powerful path to contributing joy to the world, and that practices such as prayer, meditation, study, selfless service, and giving are what make the fullness of life available to all.

I believe that the Thing Itself is limitless and extends in time and space in all directions, and I call that eternity, and I understand that any moment I am experiencing is an eternity. And I have come to learn that human forgiveness is the process that frees us to live with each other in compassion eternally.

I believe that there is something intrinsically good about people and that we are endowed with free will. And I believe that what the world calls evil is not an independent entity or force. I believe that I, together with all other people, experience, create, and further evil to the degree that we are out of alignment with ordinary goodness, and that when we come back into alignment all things are made new.

Postlude

Be Calm and Carry On

Once upon a time, students of an enlightened teacher were crossing a sea in a boat. The company was surprised by a fierce storm that churned the sea. All on board had to work to keep the boat afloat despite the fierce waves and vicious wind. The unrelenting weather wore away their courage until at last they began to lose heart, and the storm on the outside caused fear to enter into their minds and spread dread. In their panic, they seemed to be forgetting the lessons their teacher had given them about the power and supremacy of inner peace.

It's understandable, after all—waves are crashing, the wind is howling, and things don't look like they reflect inner peace at all. Were they so wrong to assume that their paths would be made safe if they followed their teacher's lessons? In their panic, they approached their teacher and found him sleeping with his head on a makeshift cushion in the stern. Alarmed at his apparent disinterest in the imminent danger, they woke the sleeping teacher and asked, "Don't you even care that we are perishing?" When the teacher finally was roused from his nap, he said to the students and to the waves, "Peace, be still!" Immediately the wind quieted down, and the sea returned to its former state of calm.

The lesson of this famous story is that there is a presence that is quietly, calmly at rest in the stern of the boat, meaning deep within your consciousness. It is beyond the reach of bad weather or unexpected changes in circumstances. It is your original goodness. I like the way Thomas à Kempis addressed it when he wrote, "Ah, Lord God, Thou holy Lover of my soul, when Thou comest into my soul, all that is within me shall rejoice. Thou art my Glory and the exultation of my heart; Thou art my hope and refuge in the day of my trouble."* Had I not had the example of my grandmother's love, I would find it difficult to believe that there is such an inner refuge to which I could return no matter how the outer storm was raging.

But I did have her example and the example of so many good-hearted people who remind me that, despite all of our progress in technology and communication, there is still nothing more powerful than ordinary goodness to connect us, to guide our choices, to deepen our faith in each other, and to declare the world a beautiful place to be.

* J. Manning Potts, *Prayers of the Middle Ages: Light from a Thousand Years* (Upper Room, 1954), 81.

Appendix

Wisdom Writing Resources

One of my hopes in writing this book is that readers might be inspired to explore the writings of great authors that stir up in us the awareness of goodness. Because advertising, social media, and television project an image of life as being entirely physical and lowly in nature, it has become essential that we undo that wrong image and replace what we have been conditioned by with something hopeful and encouraging. This becomes easier to accomplish if we make space in our lives to become fascinated with goodness by interrupting the habit of *not* noticing it. Rather than go to bed accompanied by TV's sensational news or supernormal life dramas, my hope is that readers will develop the habit of going to sleep accompanied by something from the readings below, or by a mindfulness practice. See my book *The Power of Meditation* for examples of meditative exercises. Below is a short list of works that may be suitable for contemplating goodness.

The Desiderata of Happiness: A Collection of Philosophical Poems, Max Ehrmann (New York: Crown, 1995).

The Essential Marcus Aurelius, Jacob Needleman and John Piazza (New York: Tarcher, 2008).

The God Memorandum, Og Mandino (Hollywood, FL: Frederick Fell, 1995).

How to Live in the World and Still Be Happy, Hugh Prather (York Beach, ME: Conari Press, 2011).

"If," by Rudyard Kipling, in *The Collected Works of Rudyard Kipling*, Rudyard Kipling (New York: Pergamon Media, 2015).

The Invitation, Oriah Mountain Dreamer (New York: HarperCollins, 2009).

The Lazy Man's Guide to Enlightenment, Thaddeus Golas (Encino, CA: The Seed Center, 1973).

Letters of the Scattered Brotherhood, Mary Strong (New York: HarperOne, 1991).

The Optimist Creed, Christian D. Larson (New York: Tarcher, 2012).

The Power of Awareness, Neville Goddard (New York: Tarcher, 2012).

The Power of Decision: A Step-by-Step Program to Overcome Indecision and Live without Failure Forever, Raymond Charles Barker (New York: Tarcher, 2011).

The Prophet, Kahlil Gibran (New York: Alfred A. Knopf, 1923).

The Quiet Answer, Hugh Prather (New York: Doubleday, 1982).

Tao Te Ching: The New Translation from Tao Te Ching: The Definitive Edition, Lao-Tzu and Jonathan Star (New York: Tarcher, 2001).

The Upanishads: A New Translation, Vernon Katz and Thomas Egenes, translators (New York: Tarcher/Perigee, 2015).

Good News Resources

Steven Pinker and Andrew Mack, in an article for Slate.com, "The World Is Not Falling Apart," show how, despite the troubling headlines, accurate or not, there remains a larger view of the world's trends that is worth a second look.* The number of homicides in most of the world has been sinking, and rates of rape or sexual assault are at a quarter or less of their past peaks, as is victimization of children in the United States. Democracy is rising in popularity in the world, and civilian killings point downward dramatically. This is not to say that these issues should no longer be attended to or remedied, but it is to say that there is a simultaneously valid way to understand the world, and an opportunity to acknowledge what is also working well. Indeed, balancing media consumption with positive stories may very well help to dispel the fear of ominous futures and reinvigorate hope for the world.

The authors point out that news is about things that happen, and not about the ordinary things that do not happen, such as no war breaking out or no violence committed. Steven Radelet, in *The Great Surge*,† tells how we live in a time of considerable developmental progress among the global poor, but most people believe the opposite is true. Even though a significant transformation has been under way for two decades, it is widely unnoticed and unknown. Of course, it would be irresponsible to ignore that a mind-boggling number of people still live in extreme poverty, that

---

* Steven Pinker and Andrew Mack, "The World Is Not Falling Apart," Slate, December 22, 2014, http://www.slate.com/articles/news_and_politics/foreigners/2014/12/the_world_is_not_falling_apart_the_trend_lines_reveal_an_increasingly_peaceful.single.html.

† Steven Radelet, *The Great Surge: The Ascent of the Developing World* (New York: Simon & Schuster, 2015).

millions of people die from preventable disease, and that tyranny and corruption still run rampant. Nevertheless, we have to purposefully seek out the testimony of the good that is being committed in the world and to let it infuse us with hope and courage for a greater world yet to be.

Below are some news services that focus on inspiring stories and wholesome events.

ABC News Good News (ABCnews.go.com/US/Good_News) — Inspirational and happy news stories that will make you smile and feel good.

Gimundo (Gimundo.com) — A curated collection of good news stories, inspiring videos, and original feature articles about everyday heroes, advice for green living, arts, and culture.

Globalgoodnews (GlobalGoodNews.com) — A publicly funded website that documents the rise of a better quality of life that is dawning in the world.

GoodNewsNetwork (GoodNewsNetwork.org) — A daily source for only good news, inspiring stories, and images from around the world to make you feel uplifted, optimistic, and positive about life.

HuffPost Good News (HuffingtonPost.com/Good-News) — A spotlight on what's inspiring, what's positive, and what's working, presenting the stories most media outlets choose not to cover.

OptimistWorld (OptimistWorld.com) — A website dedicated to highlighting the positive things that are happening in the world.

South Africa: The Good News (SAGoodNews.co.za) — Highlighting the stories of positive developments, progress, and hope from a remarkable nation.

Sunny Skyz Positive News (SunnySkyz.com/good-news) — Sharing only positive, upbeat media that inspires with uplifting news, inspirational stories, feel-good pictures, and videos so that you can live, laugh, and love.

Today Good News (Today.com/News/Good-News) — News, videos, and photos about good news.

Acknowledgments

Thank you to the people who supported the creation of this book—in alphabetical order, William Abel, David Coppini, Randall Friesen, Christopher Fritzsche, Kevin Krage, and Martha Salazar. Thank you for your endurance, corrections, encouragement, and suggestions.

Thank you to Joel Fotinos, Andrew Yackira, and the team at TarcherPerigee for guiding me through the completion of the project.

I am grateful for the writings of Eknath Easwaran (*Original Goodness: Strategies for Uncovering Your Hidden Spiritual Resources*), Chris Benguhe (*Beyond Courage: The 9 Principles of Heroism*), and Piero Ferrucci (*The Power of Kindness: The Unexpected Benefits of Leading a Compassionate Life*), which have inspired and informed my understanding of ordinary goodness.

ABOUT THE AUTHOR

EDWARD VILJOEN (pronounced full-YOON) is the senior minister at the Center for Spiritual Living in Santa Rosa, California. He is the author of *The Power of Meditation: An Ancient Technique to Access Your Inner Power* and the Kindle book *Bhagavad Gita for Beginners: The Song of God in Simplified Prose*, the coauthor (with Chris Michaels) of *Spirit Is Calling* and *Practice the Presence*, and the coauthor (with Joyce Duffala) of *Seeing Good at Work*. He lives in California.